STUDIES IN HISTORY, ECONOMICS AND
PUBLIC LAW

Edited by the

FACULTY OF POLITICAL SCIENCE
OF COLUMBIA UNIVERSITY

NUMBER 355

STATE-ADMINISTERED LOCALLY-SHARED TAXES

DEVELOPMENT IN THE STATE AND LOCAL TAX SYSTEMS OF THE UNITED STATES

BY

RUTH GILLETTE HUTCHINSON

To

PROFESSOR MABEL NEWCOMER

PREFACE

The relation of state tax systems to local tax systems is a problem of widespread interest at the present time. The changes that are being made in state and local functions and in state and local revenues are requiring major readjustments to harmonize state and local needs and resources. This monograph deals with the particular phase of the problem covered by legislation providing for state-administered locally-shared taxes in the United States. The study covers both the legal and financial aspects of the problem. An exhaustive analysis is presented of the growth, tendencies and influence of this phase of our tax system.

ACKNOWLEDGMENTS

THESE acknowledgments can express only in part my deep appreciation to those who have assisted me in the preparation of this document. Professor Edwin R. A. Seligman has given me valuable criticism and suggestion. Professor Robert M. Haig has been very generous of his time in making comments and suggesting new ideas, as well as in most careful supervision. Professor Mabel Newcomer has from the first given inspiration and guidance. Her sustained interest has contributed immeasurably to that which may be of value in these pages.

I wish to acknowledge the courtesy shown to me by the Librarians of the American Telephone and Telegraph Company and the Librarian of the New York State Tax Commission in allowing me to use the materials available in their libraries.

RUTH GILLETTE HUTCHINSON.

VASSAR COLLEGE, JUNE 16, 1931.

CONTENTS

CHAPTER I

INTRODUCTION

Development of Centralization in State Tax Administration

A STUDY of state and local finances of the United States during the nineteenth century reveals that the states received most of their revenue from locally-collected taxes. The local governments had a large number of locally-elected tax officials who assessed and collected the taxes for both the local districts and the states, with relatively little state supervision. Toward the end of the nineteenth century the states began to develop independent sources of revenue, and, therefore, relied less and less on locally-collected taxes. This transition, which had small beginnings in the nineteenth century, has continued at an increasing pace in the twentieth century. In 1902 fifty-two per cent of the state tax revenue was still obtained from the general property tax. In 1925 the percentage had decreased until the locally-collected property tax was only twenty-eight per cent of total state revenue. In 1928 this proportion had declined even further to twenty-five per cent of the state tax revenue.[1] The states are getting the remainder of their revenue from several different sources. Many of these sources were originally part of the older property tax base; others evolved with new methods of living and carrying on business. In 1928 the states obtained

[1] Figures for 1902 and 1925 from Newcomer "Tendencies in State and Local Finance, and their Relation to State and Local Functions," *Political Science Quarterly*, vol. 43, no. 1, March, 1928, p. 4.

Figures for 1928 from "Financial Statistics of States," *Bureau of the Census*, Washington, 1928, p. 5.

nine per cent of their tax revenue from special property taxes, eighteen per cent from motor vehicle licenses, sixteen per cent from the gasoline tax, eight per cent from the inheritance tax, four per cent from the income tax, and the rest from poll taxes and other special taxes and licenses.[1] A few of the special property taxes and poll taxes are locally-collected, but the great majority are state-administered taxes. In other words, the states are receiving their revenue largely from new state-administered taxes which have developed as the country has developed, and are, thereafter, less dependent on the locally-administered property taxes. The states have gone even further than this,—not only are they collecting the larger part of their own revenue, but they are also collecting a considerable and increasing revenue which is returned to the local districts either as a subvention or as a share of a particular tax.

A brief historical survey of the economic evolution of the United States demonstrates quite clearly the reasons for the change to state collection of revenue. In the colonial period the local units were used as tax-collecting units. These local divisions were important units of government in the colonies, and the only change at the time of the Revolution was the authorization of the local charters by the states rather than by the Crown.[2]

During the period following the Revolution these strong, almost independent, local units with popular election of local officials were founded in increasing numbers. The town was the most important local unit in New England, while elsewhere the county developed as the more powerful divi-

[1] Computed from "Financial Statistics of States," *Bureau of the Census*, Washington, 1928, p. 5.

[2] J. A. Fairlie, *Local Government in Counties, Towns and Villages*, New York, 1906, p. 33; C. C. Maxey, *Outline of Municipal Government*, New York, 1924, p. 3.

sion of local government. There was also a growth of incorporated towns, villages and boroughs as population increased. Contemporaneous with the numerical development of these local units there was an opposing development, somewhat independent, *viz.*, centralization and control of these units. During the eighteenth and early nineteenth centuries the two were not necessarily opposed, but with the passage of time the part played by the state became increasingly important, particularly in administration of taxation. The reasons for this are found in the industrial development of the country, and (so far as state administration of taxation is concerned) in considerable dissatisfaction with the early property taxes, which was only in part a result of changing economic conditions.

During the latter part of the eighteenth century and all of the nineteenth century the chief sources of both state and local revenue had been property taxes, for the United States was predominantly an agricultural nation until near the beginning of the twentieth century.

The first property taxes are entirely in harmony with the facts of early industrial life. It is a matter of common knowledge that the early period of almost every civilization is marked by two chief facts, the preponderance of agriculture and the existence of slavery. . . . In early civilization there was a quantitative, but no qualitative, distinction in wealth. Property consisted chiefly of land and the landowner's household, including slaves and beasts of burden. There was no important capital . . . apart from this landed property, and hence there were no distinct shares in distribution. . . . It was as true of the slaveholding states in the American union . . . as it was of the early Hellenic civilization. Wherever we find only agriculture and slavery, there we have this inseparable mass of collective property, not yet split into its constituent parts.[1]

[1] Edwin R. A. Seligman, *Essays in Taxation*, New York, 1925, p. 11.

The taxes in the colonies were first levied on gross produce of land. These tended to grow into taxes on real property and soon expanded into general property taxes. In addition to the property taxes there were a few other forms of taxation. All state systems were supplemented by poll taxes, licenses and excise taxes in various combinations in each state. Since there was comparatively little difficulty in reaching these bases of taxation, and since the local units already had popularly elected officials who could do the work, the states' share of the property taxes was apportioned to the various local officials for collection. These officers were given much freedom in administering the taxes. The states did not interfere with local assessments on which the states based their own tax levies. The local officers were even used for the collection of purely state taxes, such as the inheritance tax, receiving a percentage of the tax collected as a fee for collection. The period prior to 1890 has been characterized by Mr. Crobaugh as one of " administrative decentralization " of the fiscal relations of the state and local governments.[1]

In the latter part of the nineteenth century this system of state and local taxation became increasingly unsatisfactory for many reasons. During and after the Civil War the United States developed industrially at a rapid rate. Although the majority of the population was still engaged in agriculture the number of people going into trade, commerce and manufacture grew by leaps and bounds. Railroad mileage in operation increased from 30,626 miles in 1860 to 198,334 miles in 1900.[2] The capital invested in manufacture increased from a little less than one billion dollars in

[1] Crobaugh, " Centralizing Fiscal Tendencies in State and Local Relations," *National Tax Association Proceedings*, New York, 1924, p. 172.

[2] Statistical Abstract of the United States, *Bureau of the Census*, 1903, p. 396.

1860 to nine billion eight hundred million dollars in 1900.[1] This industrial development was marked by a replacement of the individual enterprise by the corporate form of organization.

During the early part of the century banks and insurance companies had been the chief types of corporate business, although turnpike and toll-bridge enterprises were often incorporated. Success in these fields encouraged the adoption of the corporate form of organization in manufacturing and railroading. In taxing this new institution the states tried to use the existing general property tax. But the local assessors were unable to cope with the problem of assessing a large part of the property of corporations, and as such property increased the evasion became serious. Furthermore, the taxation of stocks and bonds owned by individuals in addition to the taxes laid on the assets of corporations often meant double taxation.

The general property tax was particularly heavy for the farmer whose assets were visible, and comparatively easy to evaluate, while corporate excess, and the property of public utilities which was more difficult to assess, and some forms of personalty often escaped taxation. The fundamental reasons for the bitter protest against the property tax are given by Professor Seligman in his discussion of the general property tax.[2] The first of these defects is, he points out, the lack of uniformity, which is a glaring infraction of the fundamental rule of equality in taxation. The second defect is lack of universality, through the failure to reach personal property; and it is precisely in the localities where the extent and importance of personal property is greatest that its assessment is the poorest. Third, there is the incentive to dis-

[1] "Manufactures," Twelfth Census of Manufactures, *Bureau of the Census*, Washington, 1900, vol. vii, pt. i, p. xiv.

[2] Seligman, *op. cit.*, pp. 19-31.

honesty in the opportunity to evade the personal property tax. Numerous tax commissions show that this tax becomes a tax on ignorance and honesty. Fourth, the property tax tends to become regressive; that is, the rate of the tax on the full value increases as the amount of property decreases. This is because of the fact that the tax is on the property which the assessor sees, and the small farm is more likely to be assessed at its full value than the large estate. Fifth, there is double taxation if the property is taxed and the mortgage on it is also taxed. Still, if an offset is allowed for mortgages and indebtedness it often leads to tremendous injustice and deception, since much fictitious indebtedness is created to evade taxation. "There is no logical escape from one of the two methods, debt-taxation or debt-exemption; and under either plan the general property tax stands convicted by the test of experience."[1] Finally Professor Seligman insists that property is no longer a satisfactory criterion of faculty, or tax-paying capacity, and concludes "Practically the general property tax as actually administered is beyond all doubt one of the worst taxes known in the civilized world."[2]

The general protest against the property tax has brought two different lines of reform, both leading to state centralization. First, the state began to take over the supervision of assessment through a state tax commission or a state board of equalization; and secondly, new taxes were developed to reach the new forms of wealth and to tax its productivity rather than its value. The supervision of assessments has meant, necessarily, state administrative control, which has been largely in the hands of state tax boards. According to Professor Lutz:

[1] *Ibid.*, p. 31.

[2] *Ibid.*, p. 62.

The first significant step toward more efficient administration was the creation of boards of review and equalization. . . . The second step toward administrative reform, state control of corporate assessments, was occasioned by the growth of the modern corporation especially of the public service type. The farcical character of local assessment of such properties was early recognized, even by those who could see no further defects in the tax system. . . . The progressive decline of the general property tax led to the final reform, the establishment of the state tax commission. This body has usually taken over the functions of equalization and corporation assessment. Its distinctive function has been, however, the more or less effective supervision of local officials and the general administration of the entire tax system.[1]

Professor Lutz believes that it is not solely the failure of the general property tax, but also the growing complexity of civilized life, leading to the need for greater administrative control, which has brought the state tax commission.[2] The first modern state tax commission was that of Indiana in 1891. All of the states now have state tax boards or officials. All but five of these, Delaware, Idaho, Rhode Island, Texas and Vermont,[3] have some supervisory power over local-taxing officials. This line of reform of the general property tax means state control and supervision of what were formerly local tax functions.

The second reform movement which has its roots in the defects of the general property tax is the development of new forms of taxation. As early as 1823 New York had passed a special property tax for corporations. The tax was modified in 1825 and again in 1828. These amendments

[1] H. L. Lutz, *The State Tax Commission*, Cambridge, 1918, pp. 5-6.

[2] *Ibid.*, p. 636.

[3] "Federal and State Tax Systems," *New York State Tax Commission*, New York, 1930.

attempted to reach all corporate property by taxing real estate and using capital stock as the test of value of the corporate personal property. Following the early lead of New York many of the states added to the property tax some new form of corporation tax.[1] State taxation of a corporation does not necessarily remove it from local taxation, but often when a state tax is imposed, the local district is allowed to tax only the physical property.

The corporation was not the only tax subject taken over by the state for taxation. The automobile has come to be almost universally taxed by the state. State registration was necessary for regulation, and it was easier to tax it at the time of registration. The gasoline tax is a state tax. It taps a source which the localities would find difficult to administer efficiently. As with the corporation tax, these taxes frequently withdraw from local taxation certain classes of property. Many of the states have for this reason been sharing the revenue from these taxes with the localities. Today the states are receiving an increasing proportion of their revenues from state-administered taxes such as the motor vehicle and gasoline taxes, the corporation tax and the income taxes, some of which they share with the localities.

State tax administration is generally conceded to be more efficient than local administration. The state, with its wider jurisdicition, can reach effectively wealth which the local district fails to tax, either because the owner of the wealth lives outside of the local district or because the wealth itself is removed when taxes are imposed. Another reason for state administration is that central control and assessment are apt to be more impersonal and consequently more equitable than local administration. Furthermore, in the case of many taxes like the corporation taxes, local assessment means a piecemeal and, consequently, an inaccurate assessment. In

[1] Seligman, *op. cit.*, pp. 146-148.

assessing a railroad no one local district is likely to have knowledge of its value as a going concern. In such a case state assessment seems imperative.

This tendency toward centralization has brought a storm of protest from those who believe in home rule as the "cradle of American democracy". The protest is against the states' assumption of many local functions and not merely against state tax administration. This study of state-administered locally-shared taxes indicates, however, that state administration of taxation is the first step toward state control of the functions supported by these taxes. The state is increasing its control of local functions by minimum requirements. In the case of roads it may require that the road be built to satisfy the state highway commission. Minimum educational standards in the way of teachers per student and the length of the school year are often prescribed. As the amount of revenue returned grows larger the restrictions placed on the localities increase in number and rigor.

Before considering further the reasons for sharing the revenue, it is well to consider the relative proportions of total tax revenues which the state and local districts spend. In 1890, the local districts spent $487,000,000 or 86.4 per cent of the total state and local expenditures for that year. In 1927, the local districts spent only 79.6 per cent of the total state and local expenditures while the state expenditures amounted to $1,656,000,000 or 20.4 per cent of the total expenditures.[1] In spite of the increasing proportion of state expenditures the local districts still spend more than half of the total amount spent by all governmental units, and four times as much as the states spend.

[1] "Cost of Government in the United States, 1927-28," *National Industrial Conference Board*, New York, 1930, p. 2. The amounts given back to the localities are included in the figures for state expenditures.

STATE CENTRALIZATION OF FUNCTION VS. HOME RULE

From the time that the states were organized they have interfered increasingly with local governments. There are today in most states constitutional provisions which take from the state legislatures the right to make special or local laws. The limitations directly connected with the present problem are the debt limits and the tax limits imposed by the state constitutions upon municipalities. There undoubtedly does exist, as Professor Porter remarks, a regard for the American feeling for self-government and administrative decentralization.[1] The desirability of home rule centers almost entirely about the rights of the city. Are municipal functions so essentially local that the state should give the cities financial aid rather than take over the functions? The arguments in favor of retention of local functions by the cities are many. In the first place, as Professor McBain suggests, the cities are a natural unit.

> Congestion of population is the essential premise of city existence. Out of this premise arise economic and social problems that are manifestly localized. The city, in consequence, is a more or less natural unit of government. It is a far more logical unit than is a state of the American Union; it is even more logical than many of the natural units of the world. . . . It may be impossible to define with precision which of the problems of government within a city are inherently local in character. It seems, nevertheless, beyond dispute that there are problems that are peculiarly local. This is recognized to an extent in the naked fact of incorporation, in the mere investing of the city with legal personality.[2]

Another argument, as advanced by Mr. Bryce, is that

[1] K. H. Porter, *County and Township Government in the United States*, New York, 1922, p. 87.

[2] H. L. McBain, *American City Progress and the Law*, New York, 1918, p. 1.

home rule is the school for democracy; he says: "Where it [the town] is of native American stock, and the number of voting citizens is not too great for thorough and calm discussion, no better school of politics can be imagined, nor any method of managing local affairs more certain to prevent jobbery and waste, to stimulate vigilance and breed contentment."[1] This argument would not hold, however, for a unit of government larger than the town, as there is then the danger of the interests of the citizens being so diverse as to lead to factions and disputes. Furthermore, as the number of foreigners within any unit grows the advantages of home rule become more doubtful, since ignorance of the language makes these foreigners easy prey for demagogues.[2]

Professor Beard adds as a third reason for home rule the fact that state control often means that a rural legislature tries to deal with urban problems.

> The state legislature is unfitted to exercise control over matters which affect only the dwellers in large cities. It is composed mainly of countrymen or residents of small towns who are not familiar with the requirements of urban life . . . there are a number of purely municipal problems which cannot have any considerable interests for people of the state at large.[3]

On the other hand there are many arguments against home rule. The strongest of these, as Professor McBain points out, is the incapacity of the cities to rule themselves. "By and large, the capacity of the city for self-government is doubtless measured directly by our capacity as a people for creating and operating democratic institutions."[4] A second argument is that

[1] J. Bryce, *The American Commonwealth*, New York, 1922, p. 601.

[2] *Ibid.*, pp. 601-2.

[3] C. A. Beard, *American Government and Politics*, New York, 1910, p. 704.

[4] McBain, *op. cit.*, p. 4.

There are few, if any, purely municipal functions which do not have an interest for the state as a whole. If the city wishes to establish water works it must go, sometimes, as New York City has gone, a hundred miles or more into the country, and must, therefore, secure watersheds by state concession.[1]

Furthermore, state interest is involved in many health problems that are handled by the city, as health affects the whole population.

Mr. Webb brings out many more arguments against home rule. He feels that the

poorer localities need aid to prevent the cost of government falling upon them as a crushing burden; that the smaller authorities require the counsel and information of wider experience; that negligent and apathetic authorities have to be incited to bring their administration up to the national minimum that is called for by the interests of the country as a whole, and that all local authorities are better for an entirely independent audit of accounts.[2]

Another count against home rule is found in the history of graft and misrule in local finances. It is only necessary to mention the names of such cities as Chicago, New York or Philadelphia to call to mind glaring instances of such questionable practices. Local governments seem prone to exceed debt limits, make unauthorized expenditures and incur unreasonable debts, even though legal, for the next administration to pay.

Whether the localities should perform certain functions is as these arguments bring out, a question fundamentally of what is best for the people. That there is no inherent right of self government was set forth in a decision by Judge

[1] Beard, *op. cit.*, p. 704.

[2] J. W. Grice, *National and Local Finance*, London, 1910, Introduction, p. x.

Cooley in 1871 in the case of People vs. Hurlburt.[1] In commenting on the case, Judge Dillon says " It can be stated as a general proposition that, in the absence of special constitutional provision, there is no right of self-government not subject to legislative control." [2] For purposes of this paper the important question which arises from this discussion is a query as to just what a local function is. With the rapid changes in economic life it is difficult to say what is generally accepted as a local function and what is not. Many functions formerly local seem to be assuming state, if not national dimensions. The maintenance of schools was originally, to a large extent, a local function, although the national government granted land for educational use. Today, however, it has become both a state and local function. Many of the educational institutions are distinctly of state character and should be taken care of by the state revenues.[3] Again, the state is taking part by imposing certain minimum standards which drain the local treasuries. It is demanding compulsory attendance, determining general outlines of the course of study, the type of books to be used, and minimum salaries for teachers. To meet these expenses the states in most cases give some aid to the schools either as a subsidy or as a portion of certain taxes. The function is no longer exclusively locally-controlled or locally-financed.

The maintenance of public safety, originally a local function, has, with easy and rapid means of communication and transportation, become a matter of state-wide concern. Although in some cities,—Boston, St. Louis or Baltimore, for example, police control is in the hands of a commissioner or board appointed by the governor of the state, and most states

[1] 24 Michigan 41.

[2] J. F. Dillon, *Commentaries on the Law of Municipal Corporations*, Boston, 1911, p. 154.

[3] G. F. Shirras, *Public Finance*, New York, 1924, p. 87.

have a state constabulary, state control is by no means general.

Control of public works and utilities, such as streets, parks, docks, sewers, terminal facilities, gas and electric light plants, street railways, subway and elevated companies, is still largely a local function, but is becoming more and more a matter of general concern, as is shown by the numerous state public service commissions. Even charities and corrections are becoming functions over which there is state control.

More recently the planning and executing of highway systems has become a state function. Professor Maxey recommends classification of highways with the state paying for primary roads, sharing the expense on secondary roads with the local governments, and a tertiary system entirely financed by the county with the state highway department supervising all, and having the power to make necessary repairs to even the strictly local roads and to exact payment from the county for such expenditures.[1] This method assures the road-users of good through highways in towns and villages; the feeder roads, which are largely of local interest, are still a local responsibility, at least in part, but cannot be neglected, as there is state supervision.

These illustrations are sufficient to indicate that there is no clear-cut line between local and state functions. Both Professors Shirras and Bastable suggest that matters of general concern should be under the control of the central powers, while matters of local concern should be under the control of the local powers. They add that when great skill and intelligence are required, and when unity and uniformity of action are desired, central administration may give better results. If the case is one which does not demand great skill, but does involve local diversity and free adaptation to local

[1] C. C. Maxey, *County Administration*, New York, p. 158.

requirements, the local administration offers an advantage.[1] Professor Lutz, in commenting on Professor Bastable's suggestion, says that in modern economic life there is no clear demarcation between matters of general and local concern, and very often both elements are present in a given situation. He believes that other things, such as relative efficiency and relative resources, should be considered, and he adds that the task of supplying our modern public demands is so great that it requires the joint efforts and resources of central and local governments for its fulfillment.[2]

It is not the purpose of this chapter to attempt to decide whether home rule as a principle is better than state control, nor to say what are state functions and what are local; but rather to point out that here are many expensive functions which the local units are still expected to perform.

It might be more efficient to transfer some of these functions to the state for administration, in which case the jurisdiction which is most efficient in collecting the newer taxes would also be responsible for carrying out the increasing expenditures which are necessary. To transfer the expenditures merely because of inability to pay the bills seems to be a doubtful solution, and it can hardly be upheld if the political impracticability of it is considered, while so many people believe with Mr. Bryce that local government is the "school of democracy".

SOURCES OF LOCAL REVENUE

There are several ways of meeting the local need. One of the most obvious solutions would be to remove the legal restrictions in the form of debt and tax limits which the state imposes on the municipalities. The debt limit and tax

[1] C. F. Bastable, *Public Finance*, London, 1903, p. 114; Shirras, *op. cit.*, p. 88.

[2] H. L. Lutz, *Public Finance*, New York, 1924, pp. 116-8.

limit were mentioned above as phases of state control over local districts, and they are regarded by the city, county, or town officials as a serious curtailment on their powers to raise revenue. It is true that the fixed limits are the results of quite arbitrary legislation. There has been considerable agitation against tax limits wherever the revenue received under them is inadequate to satisfy local desires. This agitation has brought results. About one-half of the states in the United States have made their tax limits higher during the last decade, although they have not done away with them entirely. There are only four states, Connecticut, Maine, New Jersey and New Hampshire, which do not have any tax limits in their constitutions. Even these have them in a few of their city charters. The danger in tax limits is that they may cause the municipalities to cut expenditures arbitrarily, or to accumulate debts. However, the taxpayer feels that they are a protection against very high taxes on real estate. They have not afforded the amount of protection hoped for, but they have forced the local districts to get their revenue from a larger number of sources.[1]

In order to make it possible for the local governments to meet the increasing need for revenue, various other methods have been suggested and tried. In some cases the states have tried complete separation of sources, leaving certain sources, notably the general property tax, entirely to the locality. In some, the state has set rates for locally-administered taxes, e. g. New York mortgage tax, thereby making it possible for the local districts to use a higher rate than they could make effective if the rate were merely local. In other cases the states have been giving the local districts subsidies. Another method is to share the state-administered taxes. Most states have no single, clear-cut system, but a fusion of these four methods.

[1] Newcomer, *op. cit.*, pp. 8-9.

Separation of sources, which divides the sources of revenue between the state and locality, allowing the local districts to collect all revenue from certain sources, is principally an administrative reform. It was originally adopted to avoid the evils of the property tax. One difficulty experienced in deciding which sources should go to each authority has been that the most efficient unit for administration has not necessarily been the one which has need of the revenue, and in the United States administration and use have tended to go together. Separation has been determined largely by administrative efficiency. For this reason separation usually means that the state gives up the taxation of general property, perhaps withdrawing certain classes of corporate property or intangibles from the local tax base. Local taxation of property may not be more efficient than state, "but as long as administration and use are combined it would seem the only feasible division." [1] The following advantages are generally advanced for separation of sources: first, it would lead to home rule; second, separation is in accord with the natural division of governmental activities and follows the principle already laid down in the separation of national and state revenue; third, separation would bring improved administration, as it will remove the conflict between city and county, and would tend to equalize assessments, or at least eliminate the disadvantages of inequality; and fourth, it would equalize the burden between different types of property. The disadvantages are, first, that home rule will be encouraged, but that it is undesirable; second, that there is no relation between division of government activities and collection of taxes; third, that diversity of interest is not removed; fourth, having removed the state property tax the state has also given up state assessment, and local assessment

[1] M. Newcomer, *Separation of State and Local Revenues in the United States*, New York, 1917, p. 16.

is not satisfactory; fifth, separation leads to wastefulness when it results in a large increase in corporation taxes, since people do not feel the burden, and therefore spend more freely; and sixth, that, there is no elastic state tax.[1]

In her study in 1917 of separation of taxes in Delaware, Pennsylvania, New York, Connecticut, New Jersey, Vermont, West Virginia and California, Professor Newcomer reached the following conclusion:

> There are no advantages to be derived from complete separation of sources which cannot be derived in other ways, and there is little likelihood that it will become a permanent feature of any state's system; but as a transitional stage in the movement from the general property tax widely applied to classification for taxation it will doubtless play an important part.[2]

The California Tax Commission of 1928 reports on results in California, after a survey of separation of sources in that state from 1910 to 1928, and says: " The conclusion is inescapable that, although the adoption of the plan of separation of sources did bring about a substantial improvement as compared with the situation which existed previously, the course chosen far from being ' the one feasible pathway to tax reform ' has proved to be a blind alley ".[3]

Professor Seligman, in his consideration of fiscal relation of central and local government, discusses separation of sources as follows: " If by separation of source we mean . . . the liberation of the state from dependence on the locally assessed property tax, there can be no valid objection to it." [4] This is a broader interpretation than we have been consider-

[1] *Ibid.*, pp. 18-24.

[2] *Ibid.*, p. 191.

[3] *Final Report of the California Tax Commission*, Sacramento, March 5, 1929, p. 52.

[4] Seligman, *op. cit.*, p. 667.

ing: "But if by separation of source we mean absolutely distinct sources of revenue for central and for local purposes, with no possibility of the state sharing some of its revenue with the localities, the project is by no means beyond criticism."[1] His first objection is the fundamental one that complete separation of sources might put into too bold relief a division which does not exist in actual life, and moreover, may sometimes introduce fiscal embarassment, as the sources may yield too little in any one year to one or the other of the units. Furthermore, there is no convincing reason why the surplus of one kind of revenue should not be utilized to make good the deficit of the other. "In short, while there is much to be said for the principle of separation of sources, correctly interpreted we conclude that in the strict sense of the term it is in need of being supplemented by other principles in order to secure a well-rounded fiscal system."[2] There are, for example, many corporation taxes, particularly public utility taxes, which are more efficiently administered by the state than by the local district, and which should be, therefore, state-administered taxes. But at the same time the locality should share in the revenue from this source, since the local district needs the money, and the locality contributes to the value of such corporations.

Accepting this point of view, state-administration of locally-shared taxes may well be considered the next step following separation of sources. By this method the unit which is most efficient in levying the tax may administer it, and at the same time some rough attempt to meet state and local need may be made in the distribution of the revenue or the revenue may be retained where collected.

Before considering the state-administered locally-shared taxes in detail there are two other methods of supplementing

[1] *Ibid.*, p. 667.

[2] *Ibid.*, p. 668.

local revenues which should be mentioned: namely, locally-administered taxes for which the state fixes the rate, and subventions from the general revenue of the state. Professor Newcomer made a study of the amounts received by the localities in the United States from these two sources, and found that the proportion of total local tax revenue from state-controlled local taxes was .7 per cent in 1925, a considerably smaller proportion than in 1902 when these taxes furnished 5.2 per cent of the local tax revenue.[1] This control is necessary for uniformity in local business or occupational licenses, and in poll taxes, and makes available for the localities on an equal basis sources of taxation which would otherwise be difficult to administer. A business license tax, if high in one town and low in another, might cause the business to migrate. A state-wide control of such a tax would make this method of evasion impossible, and permit all towns to charge a higher rate than they could otherwise. Such taxes cannot, however, be considered a large or vital part of the tax system. This has been increasingly true since national prohibition has taken away the liquor tax, which was one of the most lucrative of these taxes.

Local revenues may be increased through subventions which are a larger part of local revenues than either state-administered taxes or state-controlled local taxes. However, they retain the same relative position in the tax system now as in 1902, having been 7.6 per cent of total local tax revenue in 1902 and 7.4 per cent in 1925.[2] They tend to hold their own, while state-controlled local taxes have a position of decreasing importance and state-administered taxes have a position of increasing importance. Subventions may

[1] Newcomer, "Tendencies in State and Local Finance, and their Relation to State and Local Functions," *Political Science Quarterly*, March, vol. xxxxiii, no. 1, p. 13.

[2] *Ibid.*, p. 13.

be considered dangerous by advocates of home rule,—perhaps even more dangerous than state-administered locally-shared taxes, for as Professor Newcomer points out

> The control exercised by the state through this means is often more far-reaching than the amount of money distributed indicates, since local districts are often required to achieve certain state-dictated standards at their own expense before receiving state money, and the cost of achieving these standards usually far exceeds the amount of the subvention. The subvention is, consequently, a powerful agent of control.[1]

The one other method of securing adequate revenues for the locality is the use of state-administered locally-shared taxes. These are growing in number and yield, and it is these taxes that are the central subject of this monograph.

[1] *Ibid.*, p. 23.

CHAPTER II

State-Administered Locally-Shared Taxes

DEFINITION OF STATE-ADMINISTERED LOCALLY-SHARED TAXES

In deciding just which taxes should be included in this study it has been necessary to place some rather arbitrary limitations on the definition of state-administered locally-shared taxes. The variations in methods of collection and ways of distributing the revenue were so numerous that the test had to be clearcut and definite. State-administered locally-shared taxes are taken to mean those taxes which are collected by the state and the proceeds of which are then distributed, at least in part, to the local divisions without losing their identity as the yield of specific taxes, and also those taxes which are locally-collected but over which the state has such close control that either the state checks the actual tax bills sent out, perhaps sending them out, or checks the individual receipts, even receiving the money and making the distribution to the local districts in some instances. In other words, the state is taking such an active part in the administration of the tax that lack of local interest in one locality will not let those liable to such a tax in that community escape. Thus, the motor vehicle taxes, although in many cases collected by a county official, are included if the state checks over the receipts. The Iowa license tax on those selling cigarettes is included, for although the license is issued by the city or county clerk, the state treasurer inspects the books each month and gives the stamps sold to the city clerk.[1] On the other hand, the Kansas tax on

[1] *Iowa Statutes*, 1927, ch. 78, p. 248.

" money and credits " is excluded, since the county clerk computes the tax and puts it in with the personal property tax.[1] This tax is divided between the state and county, but it is essentially a locally-administered tax. It does not meet the definition of state administration in that if a locality becomes careless in its collection, the state does not collect the tax.

Another group of taxes which it has been necessary to exclude is that group whose yield is spent for specific purposes in the locality where collected, but where the expenditure is actually made by state authorities. Such a tax is the North Carolina motor vehicle tax, where seventy per cent of the revenue is spent in the county where collected, on roads, but it is spent by the state highway commissioner.[2] If the money is given to the county to spend, the tax is included, for the county still has some control over the money returned to it even though the state checks the expenditure afterwards, as in the case of the New York motor vehicle tax, where the county spends the money " for the construction of county and town highways approved by the State Highway Commission ".[3]

These taxes differ from subventions, even when the use of the proceeds is specified in detail, in that amounts received by the local districts depend on the yield of the tax and not on some pre-determined standard of need.

Taking, then, as the test for a state-administered locally-shared tax, sufficient state supervision to insure that the tax is properly collected, together with actual local disbursement, whatever the state regulations, the author found 142 such taxes in force after the 1929 legislatures had met. The following material is based on a study of these taxes. Appen-

[1] *Kansas Statutes*, 1927, ch. 326, p. 528.

[2] *North Carolina Statutes*, 1921, ch. ii, p. 67.

[3] *New York State Statutes*, 1921, ch. 580.

dix I gives all legal citations used in studying the development of the taxes. That there were numerous changes in the bases used, in the rates levied, methods of collections, and bases for distribution will be seen from the frequent changes in the laws noted in appendix I. There were other changes which were not noted because they did not seem to have direct bearing on the present problem. The date when the tax first assumed this particular form, *i.e.*, a state-administered locally-shared tax, regardless of whether it was a new tax law or amended tax law, is used as the date of the tax throughout the present study.

THE PROBLEMS OF STATE-ADMINISTERED LOCALLY-SHARED TAXES

The number of state-administered locally-shared tax laws has increased steadily. Before 1900 there were seventeen such tax laws, most of which were on corporations. The greatest increases came from 1910 on, as the motor vehicle taxes became more important. In the last decade the largest number of cases have appeared in the gasoline taxes, and the common carrier tax is becoming more and more important. On January 1, 1930, there were in all 142 taxes which were state-administered and locally-shared.

In studying these state-administered locally-shared taxes there are certain lines of inquiry which have been uppermost in the writer's mind: First, why has the tax been returned? Second, what proportion is returned, and is this proportion tending to increase or decrease? Third, is the revenue reapportioned, *i.e.*, returned in whole or in part on some basis which distributes it to a locality other than that from which it was collected, or is it returned to the locality from which it has been collected? Fourth, does the state make special requirements when it returns this revenue? Fifth, what control is obtained through the requirements laid down for

TABLE I[a]

HISTORICAL DEVELOPMENT OF STATE-ADMINISTERED LOCALLY-SHARED TAXES, SHOWING THE DEVELOPMENT IN DIFFERENT TAXES 1900–1929

	Corporation	Inheritance	Motor Transport			Income	Forest	Severance	Miscellaneous	Total	Cumulative Total
			Motor Vehicles	Gasoline	Common Carriers						
Before 1900	13	1	—	—	—	—	—	—	3	17	17
1900–5 ...	9	2	—	—	—	—	—	—	—	11	28
1906–10 ..	6	2	—	—	—	—	—	—	—	8	36
1911–15 ..	4	2	13	—	—	1	—	1	2	23	59
1916–20 ..	7	1	6	1	2	2	—	—	2	21	80
1921–25 ..	2	1	3	13	8	1	3	3	4	38	118
1926–29 .	3	1	—	10	3	1	3	1	2	24	142
Total	44	10	22	24	13	5	6	5	13	142	

[a] The date used for these taxes is the date when they first became state-administered locally-shared taxes. (See Appendix I.) Many of them had been in force before, but had not taken on this form. Tax laws repealed before January 1, 1930, are not included.

the use of the share returned? Sixth, is the revenue substantial enough to afford the local district any relief? From these different lines of inquiry the influence of this fiscal device on the locality should be ascertained.

State-administered locally-shared taxes are increasing in number, and along with them is increasing the control of the state over local functions. The amount and proportion which they are of the local tax revenue is shown in the following table:

TABLE II [a]

PROPORTION OF STATE-ADMINISTERED LOCALLY-SHARED TAXES TO ALL LOCAL TAX REVENUE

Date	Total local tax revenue (thousands)	State administered taxes (thousands)	Percentage of state-administered taxes to total local revenue
1902	$763,372	$6,552	.9
1912	1,447,930	15,978	1.1
1925	4,581,305	186,640	4.1
1928	4,629,845	261,220	5.6

[a] Figures for 1902, 1912 and 1925 from M. Newcomer, "Tendencies in State and Local Finance and their Relation to State and Local Functions," *Political Science Quarterly*, March, vol. xxxxiii, no. 1, p. 13.
Figures for 1928 compiled from state reports and National Industrial Conference Board, *Cost of Government in the United States, 1927-8*, New York, 1930, p. 103.

For 1928 these taxes were only 5.6 per cent of all local tax revenue, but if figures for 1929 could be obtained the amount would probably be increased, for there were twelve new taxes added in 1929. The proportion that these taxes are of all local tax revenue has increased from .9 per cent in 1902 to 5.6 per cent in 1928. It is clearly a growing movement.

The total revenue from these taxes is increasing, and the source of this increase is largely new types of taxes. This is shown by the historical chart of laws and the following table of amounts and percentages of revenue by sources. In 1902 the taxes were largely corporation taxes. In 1912, although corporation taxes were still the largest single important source, the income tax and the motor vehicle tax were rapidly coming to the fore. By 1925 the gasoline tax had become another important source.

TABLE III[a]

SOURCES AND AMOUNTS OF REVENUE RECEIVED BY THE LOCAL DISTRICTS FROM THE STATE-ADMINISTERED LOCALLY-SHARED TAXES

Sources	1902	1912	1925	1928
	(in thousands of dollars)			
Total	6,552	15,978	186,640	261,220
Income tax	—	1,168	59,832	57,505[b]
Corporation tax	6,387	13,307	37,390	61,962
Tax on intangibles	—	255	417	218
Inheritance tax	165	333	720	4,612
Motor vehicle tax	—	905	58,246	67,020
Gasoline tax	—	—	28,837	64,237
Miscellaneous taxes	—	10	1,198	5,666
	(as a percentage)			
Total	100	100	100	100
Income tax	—	7.3	32.1	22.0
Corporation tax	97.5	83.3	20.0	23.7
Tax on intangibles	—	1.6	.2	.1
Inheritance tax	2.5	2.1	.4	1.8
Motor vehicle tax	—	5.7	31.2	25.7
Gasoline tax	—	—	15.3	24.6
Miscellaneous taxes	—	.1	.7	2.1

[a] Table, except for 1928, from M. Newcomer, *ibid.*, p. 18, 1928 figures compiled by the author.

[b] 1928 figure is for personal income tax only; other years include both personal and corporate income taxes.

The primary reason for returning part of the taxes to local districts is often that of political expediency. As new state tax laws are passed especially those such as some of the income tax laws, which take from the local district possible sources of taxation, the local districts demand compensation. Professor Adams recognized this in his article advocating the income tax in Wisconsin. He first expresses regret at the necessity of suggesting a method of apportionment other than upon the basis of equalized real estate values, and continues " But it is probably true that some little modification of the latter method will have to be made in order to secure the consent of the rural districts to a reform of the general property tax."[1] Although this suggestion was not adopted in Wisconsin it has been used in Massachusetts. The 1916 income tax law of Massachusetts provided for the distribution of proceeds to the local districts in proportion to losses of revenue, but in 1919 a new law provided for a gradual reduction of the amount of revenue returned as compensation for loss and an increasing amount of revenue returned in proportion to the state tax levy.[2] This particular reason for returning taxes is especially common in the cases of the corporation, income and motor vehicle taxes, most of which are from sources which were formerly part of the basis of the general property tax. In the case of motor transportation taxes the local district has a strong case on the basis of benefit conferred in road building and maintenance.

Back of the political pressure used by the local districts to get a share in these taxes is the great need for increasing revenue, caused by the increasing costs of government and expanding governmental functions. The amount of the local property tax is already, in most districts, a cause of continual dissatisfaction on the part of the taxpayers, so that the local districts must look elsewhere for funds. The possibilities of borrowing are restricted by debt limits, and the local sources of taxation are few. Consequently the local districts turn to the state for aid.

Whether the revenue returned is a substitute for former revenue or is to meet growing local needs, it is seldom proportionate to the needs of the municipalities, and involves all the dangers of local extravagance. This is particularly true

[1] Adams, "The Income Tax as a substitute for the Property Tax on Certain Forms of Personalty in the State of Wisconsin," *National Tax Association Proceedings*, vol. iv, Ohio, 1910, p. 105.

[2] *Statute Laws of Massachusetts*, 1919, ch. 314, p. 296.

of the inheritance tax, which is in eight out of ten cases returned where it is collected. The fact that the return from this tax is irregular emphasizes the danger of foolish local expenditure. However, of the revenue collected in 1928 only $80,048,000 is returned where collected, and $181,172,000 is reapportioned in an attempt to meet local needs. There are seventy-one taxes reapportioned, twenty-five of which are corporation taxes, twenty-two gasoline taxes, and eleven common carrier taxes. There is some reapportionment of the other taxes, but not as much as with these. The states seem to reapportion the tax regardless of whether the states are returning it as compensation for loss of local revenue, as in the case of the corporation taxes, or whether it is as an aid for functions for which the state is assuming some responsibility. The number of reapportioned taxes in the whole motor transportation group is thirty-seven. The fact that some of the motor transportation taxes have again changed form and are at present state taxes entirely indicates that the state administration with local sharing is a step toward full state control over the functions for which it is now subsidizing the local governments.

The basis which is most used for reapportionment is some measure of need for roads. The total returns from twenty-six taxes and part of the returns from five more were reapportioned on some measure of need for roads. All of these taxes are motor transportation taxes. Educational need was the basis for reapportionment of four taxes. Revenue for schools is usually given to the localities by subventions rather than by dividing the yield of specific taxes, since educational expenditure does not yield a special benefit to a particular group which can be reached by a specific tax. Location of the specific classes of property taxed is the basis used for sixteen and a part of one other of the taxes returned. This is reapportioned in the sense that the money is not returned to the county in which the tax is collected, but where the property itself is located. This is the basis of reapportionment for most of the corporation taxes. The returns from nine taxes, and part of the revenue of four others, are based on assessed valuation of the local districts. Each basis used for reapportionment has some good points and some disadvantages.

In apportioning the revenue according to various needs, the states have used different criteria of need. In some cases the area of the county as compared to the area of the whole state is used; in some cases the population of the county as compared to the population of the state; and in most cases of road taxes, the mileage of roads in the county as compared with total miles of roads in the state. The area of the county seems to be a very crude measure of any need. To a considerable extent population or motor vehicle registration seems to be a much better measure of the need for roads, and perhaps mileage is an even better measure.

The second method of reapportioning revenue is according to the location of the property taxed. This method bases its appeal on the fact that it returns the revenue to the county which could have reached the property itself, even though it might not have done it so efficiently. One difficulty lies in the fact that the railroad tracks, telegraph or telephone wires (which are used as bases of apportionment) may run through territory where the population is small and the needs few. Another difficulty is that of allocating the property, especially in the case of intangible property.

The third method of reapportionment is based on the assessed valuation of taxable property in each locality. Here the state is definitely attempting what was hoped for in separation, an increase of local assessment to full one hundred per cent. Separation was not successful, but as the inducement is greater in division of yield it may become helpful in raising local assessments. It has had, however, only a slight effect in helping to equalize the assessments in New York State in spite of the fact that the fifty per cent return from the personal income tax has been on the basis of assessed value of real estate since 1919. The Special Joint Committee on Taxation and Retrenchment found in 1922 that there were seventeen towns with equalization rates of 11 per cent to 20 per cent, and one hundred eighty with equalization rates below 51 per cent, whereas there were only twenty-eight with rates over 90 per cent.[1] Mr. Compton, studying the New York tax system in 1929, finds the situation little changed.[2] Whether it accomplishes the end in view or not, it is state interference with the local function of assessment.

Many of the new taxes make specific requirements for the use of the revenue. There are seventy-six tax laws which designate the use of the revenue, and in 1928 they controlled revenues of $159,907,000, or 61.2 per cent of state-administered locally-shared taxes. Twelve of these taxes are corporation taxes, fifty-five are motor transportation taxes, and four are severance taxes. Taxes returned for a function in which the state is interested tend to have specific requirements as to their use. All but four of the motor transportation taxes are restricted, whereas only twelve of the forty-three corporation taxes are allocated for a specific use. Political expediency in passing motor transportation taxes may explain this.

The fact that so much of the revenue which is returned has definite requirements for expenditures indicates that the states, at least, think there are dangers in returning free revenue. The revenue may well lead to local extravagance,

[1] *New York State Joint Legislative Committee on Taxation and Retrenchment*, Albany, 1922, p. 115.

[2] R. T. Compton, "Fiscal Problems of Rural Decline," *Special Report of the State Tax Commission*, Albany, 1930, p. 98.

particularly when reapportioned. It is well to note that this tendency to provide for the use of the returned revenue is definitely state control over the local functions. In cases where the revenue is small this is not serious, as the state revenue may be used for the designated purpose, and the local revenue which would have been so used is freed for other local needs. But if the amount returned to the districts with designated uses is large it can only mean increasing state control of functions which were formerly local.

In order to determine the effect which the movement is having on the local units each state-administered locally-shared tax has been studied separately. The theory and history of the tax is given in the chapters following in so far as it has any bearing on the present problems. The reason for return is discussed, and the proportion and amount returned, as well as the basis on which the return is made, are presented.

CHAPTER III

State-Administered Locally-Shared Corporation Taxes

The failure of the general property tax to meet the problem of reaching intangibles has become more important as the corporation has developed in the United States. Should the corporation be taxed and the securities exempted? Or should both be taxed? And just how could the corporation's personal property best be reached? Taxation of the franchise, taxation of corporate excess and taxation even of the real property when it extended through many local taxing districts became problems requiring for their solution a wider assessment jurisdiction than the local district.

At first it was assumed that the corporation could be assessed and taxed under the general property tax by local officials. New York, in 1823, passed the first law which mentioned the corporation specifically as coming under the general property tax. This law was modified in 1825 and 1828 to make it conform more closely to the general property tax. Corporations were classified and allowed various substitutions for the tax depending on the class of the corporation. In general the real estate was taxed and in addition there was a property tax on capital stock paid in, or secured to be paid in, with the amount paid on real estate and the stock owned by state or charitable institutions deducted. In all the other states which taxed corporations separately except Pennsylvania the same idea of adapting the property tax to corporations prevailed.[1]

[1] Seligman, *op. cit.*, pp. 145-148.

But this method was open to all of the difficulties of the general property tax, and hence it was gradually modified by many of the states.

The movement away from this original position has taken three directions: (1) the property of transportation companies, especially railroads, has been assessed separately; . . . (2) certain classes of corporations, beginning with banks and insurance companies, but gradually including the so-called public service corporations and in not a few cases other corporations, have been taxed, not on their property, but on certain elements supposed to represent roughly their taxable capacity; (3) all corporations in general have been taxed by a uniform rule, according to principles varying more or less in the different commonwealths.[1]

As this new movement developed different measures of taxation were used. In taxing corporations by the property tax it became necessary to develop new methods to reach the value of the franchise. In taxing public utilities special taxes were made to fit the peculiar elements of each type of corporation; for example, taxes proportional to miles of wire of telephone and telegraph companies and to amount of premiums of fire insurance companies. And in the general corporation tax various measures, such as capital stock, earnings, or dividends, have been used as the basis of taxation.

Professor Seligman reduces all of the various methods of taxing corporations to three groups; the taxes on property, which include value of property, cost of property, capital stock at par value, capital stock at market value, capital stock and bonded debt at market value, capital stock plus total debt, both funded and floating, bonded debt, or loans and capital stock according to dividends; the taxes on business, which are on business transacted as shown by deposits (in

[1] *Ibid.*, pp. 148-9.

the case of savings banks), tonnage mined (in the case of coal companies), and so on; and the taxes on net earnings, gross earnings and dividends. There are also the corporation organization taxes and franchise taxes. Different forms of taxation are used in different states for various types of corporations, and as yet there seems to be little agreement as to which are the best methods to use.

This brief summary indicates the different theories upon which corporation taxation is based. The corporation is taxed on its property and is often taxed in excess of the property on the theory that it receives special rights and privileges from the state. These two theories are both basic to the franchise tax. Professor Seligman classifies the franchise tax into three groups of franchises "the franchise to be, the franchise to do, and the franchise to act in a particular way, or to enjoy a special privilege." [1] The value of the franchise is measured in various ways, but whether the state taxes the corporate franchise as measured by property or by income, the need of state administration is evident.

The local district may still tax the corporation under the local property tax on its real estate and add a local franchise tax to the state franchise or use some other local methods of taxation. Or it may depend for its share of revenue from the corporation on a share of the state tax. For in so far as the states do, in their various tax laws, take from the locality a portion of the property of the corporation which the local district might tax, it would seem just to have a portion of these taxes returned to the local districts. Whether from a sense of justice or from political motives, forty-four of the corporation taxes in force in the various states provide for such a sharing of these taxes.

[1] *Ibid.*, p. 226.

TABLE IV

PRESENT STATUS OF STATE-ADMINISTERED LOCALLY-SHARED CORPORATION TAX LAWS, 1929[b]

State	Law first dividing revenue	Jurisdiction administering	Designated use	Percentage to local district	Basis of distribution
Alabama	Capital stock tax 1919	State Tax Commission	..	10 to counties	Proportion of taxable property of corporations in the counties where corporation does business
Arkansas	Foreign fire insurance companies 1921	Insurance Commission	Firemen's relief and pensions	50 to cities, towns and villages	Where collected
Colorado	Foreign fire insurance companies 1917	State Auditor	Firemen's pensions	50 to cities and towns	Proportion population, each city to all cities
Connecticut	Bank and insurance companies 1901	State Treasurer	..	100 to towns	Residence of shareholders-non-residents to town where bank is
Florida	Railroad companies 1907	State Comptroller	..	50 to counties	Proportion of railroad track in each county
	Telegraph companies 1907	State Comptroller	..	50 to counties	Proportion miles telegraph lines per county
	Express companies 1903	State Comptroller	..	50 to counties	Assessed valuation
Kansas	Foreign fire insurance companies 1895	State Insurance Commissioner	Firemen's fund	97 to cities and towns	Where collected
Louisiana	Foreign fire insurance companies 1914	State Treasurer	Fire departments	100 to cities and towns	Where collected

[b] Laws examined through the meetings of the 1929 legislatures.

TABLE IV—*Continued*

State	Law first dividing revenue	Jurisdiction administering	Designated use	Percentage to local district	Basis of distribution
Maine	Railroad companies 1874	County, supervised by State	..	1 per cent value of stocks held in the towns	Residence of stockholders
	Telephone and telegraph companies 1880	County, supervised by State	..	1 per cent value of stocks held in the towns	Residence of stockholders
Mary-land	Savings banks 1888	State Tax Commission	..	75 to counties	Where collected
	Capital stock tax 1914	State Tax Commission	..	50 to counties or cities	Residence of shareholders[a]
Massa-chusetts	Corporation income 1919	Commissioner of Corporations and Taxation	..	83⅓ to cities and towns	Situs of tangible property of corporation
	Public utilities 1865	Commissioner of Corporations and Taxation	..	100 on shares owned in cities and towns	Railway companies—assessed valuation; others—residence of stockholders
	Bank tax 1925	Commissioner of Corporations and Taxation	..	100 on shares owned in cities and towns	Residence of shareholders
Michigan	Steamship companies 1911	State Auditor	..	100 to counties[c]	Port of hail
Minne-sota	Steamship companies 1895	State Treasurer	..	50 to counties	Port of hail
	Domestic and foreign fire insurance companies 1903	State Treasurer	Firemens' fund	100 to cities and towns	Where collected
	Railroad companies 1909	State Treasurer	..	100 to taxing districts	Where business is transacted
Missouri	Foreign fire insurance companies, 1895	State Treasurer	Schools	50 to counties[c]	Number of schools in county

[a] If no capital stock is issued or outstanding, county share goes to the county or city where the principal office of the company is located.

[c] Divided again.

TABLE IV—*Continued*

State	Law first dividing revenue	Jurisdiction administering	Designated use	Percentage to local district	Basis of distribution
New Hampshire	Domestic and foreign fire insurance companies 1887	Tax Commission	..	75 to towns	Shares held in town
	Railroad and telegraph companies 1878	Tax Commission	..	25 to towns	Shares held in town
	Savings banks 1878	Tax Commission	..	100 to towns	In proportion to deposits in towns
	Building and loan associations 1903	Tax Commission	..	100 to towns	Where association is located
New Jersey	Railroad companies 1906	State Board of Taxes	Schools	66⅔ to counties from tax on main stem and franchise [c]	Proportion of real and personal property in county
	Public utilities except railroads 1900	State Board of Taxes	..	100 to taxing districts	Property of company on highways
	Additional public utilities except railroads 1919	State Board of Taxes	..	100 to taxing districts	Property of company on highways
New Mexico	Domestic and foreign fire insurance companies 1905	Insurance Department	Fire protection fund	100 to counties cities and towns	Proportioned to population of each jurisdiction
New York	Income of corporations 1917	State Tax Commission	..	33⅓ to counties [e]	Where tangible personal property of corporation is located; if no tangible personal property, where principal office is located
	Savings banks 1926	State Tax Commission	..	100 net of domestic banks to counties, New York City and Buffalo	New York or Buffalo or county where principal office is found
	National banks 1926	State Tax Commission	..	100 to counties, New York City and Buffalo [e]	New York or Buffalo or county where principal office is found

[e] Divided again.

TABLE IV—*Continued*

State	Law first dividing revenue	Jurisdiction administering	Designated use	Percentage to local district	Basis of distribution
North Carolina	Building loan associations 1919	Insurance Commission	..	25 to counties 25 to towns	Where association is located
North Dakota	Domestic and foreign fire insurance companies 1887	Insurance Commission	Fire departments	80 to cities, towns and villages	Where collected
Oklahoma	Foreign fire insurance companies 1909	Insurance Commission	Firemens' relief	100 to cities and towns	Where collected
Pennsylvania	Foreign fire insurance companies 1895	Insurance Commissioner	..	100 to cities and towns	Where collected
South Carolina	Foreign insurance companies 1909	Insurance Commissioner	..	50 to counties	Where collected
South Dakota	Domestic and foreign fire insurance companies 1887	State supervision of County collection	Fire departments	100 to cities and towns	Where collected
Washington	Bank tax and financial corporations 1929	Tax Commission	..	Counties*	In same proportion that personal property tax is distributed
Wisconsin	Street railways and other city utility companies 1905	State Tax Commission	..	20 to counties 65 to cities, towns and villages	Where business is located
	Telephone companies 1905	State Treasurer	..	85 to cities or towns and villages	Where exchange is located
	Corporation income 1911	State Tax Commission	..	10 to counties 50 to cities and towns	Where collected
	Foreign fire insurance companies 1920	Insurance Commissioner	Fire departments	100 to cities and towns	Where collected
Wyoming	Express companies 1903	State Auditor	..	50 to counties	Proportion of miles of line

* Divided again.

The corporation tax laws were the earliest tax laws to share revenue with the local districts, thirteen such laws having been passed before 1900. (See Table I, Chapter 11). The movement is still going on, as New York in 1926 passed two bank taxes which it shares with the localities, and Washington in 1929 passed a bank tax which it shares with the local districts.

The types of corporations whose taxes are shared vary, but the predominating kinds are the fire insurance companies and the public utilities. Fourteen of these laws are specifically for public utilities and fourteen are for fire insurance companies. But there are also seven bank taxes, two building and loan association taxes, five general corporation taxes (three on income and two on capital stock), and there are two such laws for steamboat corporations. The earliest state corporation taxes to be shared locally to any considerable extent were the public utility taxes. The reason for sharing the revenue might well be that much of the benefit for which any corporation is taxed comes from the local district which it serves, and therefore a portion of the tax is rightfully its own. In the sharing of all the corporation taxes except the fire insurance companies there is the added reason that in taxing these corporations the state has taken from the locality the right to tax tangible or intangible personalty previously subject to local taxation, and has had to make amends for what it has taken. In the sharing of the fire insurance taxes there is still another reason. These taxes are largely on foreign fire insurance companies, so that it is a source which only the state can reach adequately, and it is returned to the cities and towns to help the fire companies which are specifically a benefit to the corporations taxed.

The proportion which goes back is usually at least fifty per cent of the tax. Only three taxes, the Alabama capital stock tax, the New Hampshire railroad and telegraph tax, and the New York domestic and foreign corporation income tax, return less than fifty per cent to localities. There are twenty taxes which return between ninety-nine per cent and fifty per cent, and eighteen taxes which provide for one hundred per cent return to the local districts. The Maine railroad and telephone and telegraph taxes cannot be put into any of the above classifications, as the return varies,—one per cent of the value of the stock of these companies held in the towns being returned to such towns. Nor does the Washington bank stock tax fit into the above classification, for it is divided between the state and the municipalities in which the bank has its principal office in proportion to the amount of the personal property tax which each of these jurisdictions receives. The share of the revenue is, then, a very substantial one, giving the localities the larger portion of these taxes which are shared. In 1928 the states returned $61,962,000 to the local districts from corporation taxes out of a total of $370,000,000 collected.[1] This was more than one per cent of total local taxes received from all sources, and 23.7 per cent of all state-administered locally-shared taxes. These taxes are among the most important, as well as the earliest, of the taxes to be state-administered and locally-shared.

The proportion which goes back has been changed, in only a few cases. In the North Carolina building and loan association tax the proportion returned has been reduced from two-thirds to one-half. As the rates have gone up a little it may not mean less revenue for the locality. Another case where the proportion of the revenue returned has been decreased is the Wisconsin income tax on both personal and corporation income, which has reduced the share returned to

[1] Financial Statistics of States, *Bureau of the Census*, Washington, 1928, pp. 17, 64.

the local districts from ninety per cent to sixty per cent. In this case the basic rates used remained the same although there have been soldier and educational bonus surtaxes and there is now a teachers' retirement fund surtax with a maximum rate of one per cent. Except for this small surtax the yield from the tax is increased only by new corporations and persons paying the tax, or old taxpayers paying on larger incomes, hence, the revenue returned to the cities and towns is less. When changes are made in the proportion returned they seem to favor the state rather than the local districts, but the few changes which have actually occurred hardly justify any generalization.

The proportion going back to the localities does not tend to follow the general rule laid down by the committee appointed by the National Tax Association to prepare a plan of a model system of state and local taxation. The committee suggests in section twenty-eight of that report that:

> The proceeds of the proposed business tax may well be divided between the state and local authorities in due proportions. Our recommendation is that the states retain a proportion corresponding to that which state revenues or expenditures bear to the total state and local expenditures or revenues, and that the remainder should be turned over to the taxing district in which the business is carried on. The details of the plan of distribution may well vary from state to state, but this general rule seems to us a satisfactory general guide.[1]

The proportions given back certainly " vary from state to state ", but without any apparent relation to the proportion of state to local expenditures.

The basis for return does not follow regularly that sug-

[1] " Preliminary Report of the Committee Appointed by the National Tax Association to prepare and plan a Model System of State and Local Taxation," *National Tax Association Proceedings*, vol. xii, New York, 1919, p. 456.

gested by the Committee, for there are many states which do not turn over the local share to the taxing district where the business is carried on. The return may be made to the locality where it was collected, or it may be reapportioned. Practically all of the fourteen insurance company taxes are returned where collected. There are four exceptions. One is the New Hampshire insurance tax, which is returned on the basis of situs of shares held, but as this is a tax on capital stock it may be regarded as a tax on intangible personalty returned to the residence of the owner. In the second case, Missouri, the tax on foreign fire insurance companies is returned, not where collected, but on the basis of the number of school children. In the other two cases, Colorado and New Mexico, it is divided in proportion to population. The situation with the fire insurance companies is still different. Since most fire insurance companies are organized in Connecticut and operate in other states as foreign corporations, the taxation of most of the fire insurance companies outside of Connecticut is a problem of taxation of foreign corporations. In order to tax the premiums of all of the branches at an equal rate it is necessary to have state taxation. State taxation allows a higher tax than would be possible if the local districts competed among themselves in taxing these corporations. However, since fire protection is largely provided by the local fire departments, it seems just that at least part of the revenue should be returned to the local districts.

Some of the bank taxes, such as those of Maryland, New Hampshire, and the two New York taxes are returned where the bank is located as compensation for the property exempted. The New Hampshire and North Carolina building and loan association taxes are returned where the associations are located. The other bank taxes are reapportioned. In Washington revenue is returned in proportion to the personal property tax received and in Connecticut and Massachusetts it is returned to the residence of the owner of the stock. In the New York law, however, there is apparently also the idea of raising assessed valuations, for the counties are required to reapportion the tax among the taxing districts according to the assessed valuation of the taxing districts. The Wisconsin corporation income tax is not redivided, but goes to the cities and towns where it is assessed and collected. The two state taxes on steamship companies are also returned where the business is conducted, as they go to the counties or towns of the ports of hail. This makes nineteen of the forty-four locally-shared taxes which go back to the original jurisdictions.

There are, however, including the two bank taxes mentioned above as reapportioned, twenty-five corporation taxes where the local share of the tax is reapportioned. There are two outstanding methods for returning these shares. One way is to return the tax to the jurisdiction where the property is located instead of to the place where collected, which seems to be a logical method if the tax is returned to the local district to compensate for the property tax which might have been levied. Most of the public utility taxes, e.g., the Florida telegraph and railroad, the Maine railroad, telephone and telegraph, the Massachusetts telegraph, telephone and railroad, the Minnesota railroad, the New Hampshire railroad and telephone, the Wisconsin telephone and street railway, the Wyoming express, the New Jersey railroad taxes (*i.e.*, the portion of the tax which is on the property not used for railroad purposes), are returned to local districts in proportion to various measures of property of the company in each locality. The Alabama capital stock tax on all corporations and the Massachusetts corporate income tax are also returned where the property of the corporation is situated.

The second method of reapportioning the tax is according

to assessed valuation of taxable property, and is undoubtedly partly for the purpose of encouraging fully assessed valuations. The Florida express company tax of 1903, the Maryland capital stock tax, divided in 1914, the two New Jersey public utility corporation taxes, divided in 1900 and 1919 and the New Jersey railroad tax on the main stem and the tangible property, divided in 1906, are all of this type. These are the newer corporation taxes, and would seem to indicate that although the older taxes do not change the basis for redistribution, the desirability of bringing up assessed valuation is recognized in the passage of the new locally-shared taxes. The states seem to be taking an increasingly active part in local affairs through reapportioning these corporation taxes.

Another significant development in the same direction is the increasing attempt to set minimum standards. This is most noticeable in the return of taxes for fire departments. Since 1900 practically all taxes shared from insurance have been designated specifically for firemens' pensions or more efficient fire departments. The minimum standards set for a city or town to get this revenue have increased to include an organized fire department, usually with an apparatus of a certain value or a fire or chemical engine. In Wisconsin the law prescribes a minimum of ten active members of the department. All of these demands have been added in spite of the fact that the rate and proportion returned is the same as it always has been for this tax.

The other tax where use is prescribed for the returned share is the Wisconsin income tax, divided in 1911. If the share returned is more than two per cent of the assessed valuation of the town, the surplus is to be divided among all cities and towns of the state according to the school population, and in each city $175,000 is to go for firemen.

There seems to be a decided tendency for the state to control to a limited extent the functions of the localities through the share of the corporation taxes returned. It is not as definite a trend as in some other forms of taxation, but may point the way to the further development of state-administered locally-shared taxes.

CHAPTER IV

State-Administered Locally-Shared Inheritance Taxes

"The inheritance tax today scarcely needs defense. It is found in almost every country; and the more democratic the country, the more developed is the tax."[1] In the United States the inheritance tax has been used extensively by the states, as well as by the national government. The present United States federal tax which allows deduction of the state tax up to eighty per cent of the federal tax makes it most advantageous for the state to have a tax at least equal to the federal credit. Otherwise it is giving up revenue to the national government which might as well belong to it. There are only three states, Alabama, Florida and Nevada, which do not have inheritance taxes as part of their state systems. Nevada did have such a tax, but repealed it in 1925. Florida and Alabama have not had inheritance taxes in the twentieth century.

The inheritance tax started as a tax merely on collateral heirs, but is now extended in many states to cover direct heirs as well. The rates of many of these taxes went up during the war and have tended to stay up, so that in 1928 the inheritance tax yielded $127,538,301, or 8 per cent of the total state taxes.[2]

Professor Seligman states that the best defense of the inheritance tax is that any addition by inheritance to the wealth

1 Seligman, *op. cit.*, p. 137.

2 National Industrial Conference Board, *op. cit.*, pp. 95-7.

of the individual increases his ability to pay taxes, and the best test of faculty is revenue of the individual. This chance increase in his revenue increases his tax-paying ability. Another strong defense which has been used for centuries is that the individual should pay for the privilege of inheritance.

> The accidental income argument regards the inheritance tax as a personal tax; the privilege-of-inheritance theory regards it as an impersonal tax. . . . The one theory results in the imposition of the tax on the share of the recipient; the other theory, while possibly leading to the same result, is a tax susceptible of being interpreted as involving the imposing of the tax on the estate as a whole. The logical defense for the inheritance tax is thus the accidental-income argument as supplemented by the privilege-of-inheritance argument.[1]

Although there is nothing in the justification of the tax which gives the local districts a claim to a share in this source, some of the inheritance taxes are shared with the local districts.

Most of the state taxes are taxes on the share of the estate received, although a few states, such as Rhode Island, use both types of tax, and a few, as New York, have an estate tax. The earliest state laws on inheritance taxes were Pennsylvania, 1826, Maryland, 1845, Delaware, 1869, West Virginia 1887, and Connecticut, 1889.[2] All together, today, there are forty-five state inheritance taxes, ten of which are state-administered and locally-shared. The dates when these laws provided for state-administered locally-shared taxes range from 1894 for Ohio to 1929 for Idaho. There was one before 1900, and there have been nine since. This would indicate a gradual change which is still in progress.

[1] Seligman, *op. cit.*, p. 136.

[2] *Ibid.*, p. 137, note.

TABLE V

PRESENT STATUS OF STATE-ADMINISTERED LOCALLY-SHARED INHERITANCE TAX LAWS, 1929

State	Law first dividing revenue	Jurisdiction administering	Designated use	Percentage to district	Basis of distribution
Idaho	1929	County supervised by State	..	10 to counties	Where collected
Kansas	1909	Inheritance Tax Commission	..	5 to counties	Where collected
Louisiana	1904	Parish, supervised by State	Schools	100 to parishes	Number of school children 6 to 12 years of age
Minnesota	1911	State Treasurer	..	10 of tax paid by estates of decedents within county	Where collected
Montana	1923	State or County Treasurer	Schools	50 to counties[a]	School needs
New Jersey	1909	County supervised by State	..	5, tax paid by estates of decedents within counties	Where collected
North Dakota	1917	County supervised by State	..	65 of tax paid by estates of decedents in counties	Where collected
Ohio	1894	County supervised by State	One-half for sinking fund of municipal corporations. One-half for general revenues	50 to cities and towns	Where collected
South Dakota	1913	County supervised by State	..	10 of tax paid by estates of decedents in counties	Where collected
Wisconsin	1903	County supervised by State	..	7½ to counties	Where collected

[a] Divided again.

For the most part there seems to be little reason why the inheritance tax should be shared with the municipalities. There is one state, Kansas, where the amount returned to the county is given as a fee for aid in performing a state function. The Kansas inheritance tax has been in the past a locally-administered tax, but at present this law comes under the definition of a state-administered locally-shared tax. Although the county sends out the bill and collects the money, the inheritance tax commissioner audits the bills and no executor is allowed to consider the tax final until it has been approved by the state tax commissioner. The county "retains five per cent for the use of the county, as compensation to the county for the services the county offers." [1]

There are seven states, Ohio, Wisconsin, South Dakota, North Dakota, Minnesota, New Jersey and Idaho, which give a share to the county where the decedent formerly lived for the use of the county. This may be in the nature of a fee, but in these seven cases no such statement is made. For instance, the Idaho tax, which became a locally-shared tax in 1929, has sections in the law which insist on very close supervision by the state auditor who has "full power and authority to administer and enforce the law", and allows the county to retain 10 per cent of the yield "for the current expenses of the county".[2]

There are two states where the law aims to improve local educational standards. Montana and Louisiana reapportion the tax according to educational needs, thereby aiding the poorer counties and parishes. The inheritance tax, however, is still in most states a locally-administered state tax, and in such cases as it has become a state-administered locally-shared tax there seems to be no special reason for sharing it.

[1] *Kansas Statutes*, 1917, ch. 319, p. 469.

[2] *Idaho Statutes*, 1929, ch. 243, p. 469.

The proportions returned vary widely. Six of the states return ten per cent or less, three, Ohio, North Dakota and Montana, fifty per cent or more, and one, Louisiana, returns one hundred per cent to the parishes. The total amount of inheritance tax revenue shared with the localities in 1928 was $4,612,000, or 1.8 per cent of all state-administered locally-shared taxes. The amount the localities receive from this source is increasing, as in six out of the ten taxes being considered the proportion has remained the same in spite of the fact that the state rates have been raised, mostly by increasing the steepness of the graduation. In three states the proportion returned has itself been raised. North Dakota and Ohio have doubled the proportion returned, and in Kansas it has increased, although not as much as in the other two. South Dakota is the only state to decrease the proportion returned. If any generalization can be made from the three cases where relative amounts going to the localities have been changed, it would be that the tendency of the state is to share this source of revenue to a greater extent.

Only two of the states reapportion the revenue which is returned. The other eight return it to the county or city or town where the tax originates, *i.e.*, where the decedent formerly lived. Louisiana and Montana, both of which use the revenue for schools, reapportion according to educational needs. In Montana the state divides revenue among the counties in proportion to the number of teaching positions in which teachers were employed for a period of at least four months during the preceding year. The county superintendents divide it again among the schools in each county. In Louisiana the revenue is divided among the parishes according to the number of children between six and eighteen years of age. The poorer localities are decidedly aided by these two laws, and thus there is some state intervention.

In prescribing the purposes for which the revenue is to be

used there are three cases where the state does interfere to a considerable extent. Ohio at first merely returned the tax where collected, but in 1919 the regulation became more specific, and the money is returned to the city or town where the tax originates, one-half to be used for the sinking fund of town or city and one-half for general purposes. Louisiana merely prescribes the use of the money for schools, but in Montana the counties must divide the revenue according to this very definite formula:

Within ten days after receiving notice from the state treasurer of the apportionment made to his county, the county superintendent of schools must apportion the same as follows: sixty per cent among the several school districts, district high schools and county high schools in proportion to the total number of teaching positions in which teachers were employed for at least four months during the preceding school year; [This is the basis for the original county distribution] thirty-five per cent among the several school districts, district high schools and county high schools in proportion to the aggregate number of days attendance of all eligible pupils who attended for a period of not greater than six weeks during the preceding school year in each district school, district high school and county high school; five per cent among the district high schools and county high schools in proportion to the number of years of accredited high school work in each such district high school and county high school.[1]

The rest of the states return the revenue with no other qualification than " for the use of the county " or " for the general funds of the county ".

In the state-administered locally-shared inheritance taxes we find a few which reapportion the proceeds. The reapportionment of the tax according to educational needs appears in some instances. The dictation of use of revenue in Montana prescribes exactly the minimum amount to be spent

[1] *Montana Statutes*, 1923, ch. 65, p. 165.

in the local districts of Montana. These few instances may be added to the state-administered locally-shared taxes which show increasing state control, although by far the larger number of the inheritance taxes have no such provisions. It is, however, additional revenue for the counties in that it is a source which they could not hope to tax, and imposes so little in the way of standards.

It is questionable whether a tax from which the returns are so irregular should be shared. The report of the model tax system regards the inheritance tax as a proper source of state revenue only.[1] When it is shared it may well lead to local extravagance in the use of it, as the amount of the return is so irregular. There seems to be little justification either in the theory of the tax or in the practical results from it which should make it a tax adaptable to this form of administration, except, perhaps, a small amount as a fee for local collection.

[1] "Preliminary Report of the Committee of the National Tax Association on a Model Tax System," *National Tax Association Proceedings*, vol. xvi, New York, 1923, p. 39.

CHAPTER V

State-Administered Locally-Shared Motor Transportation Taxes

MOTOR VEHICLE TAXES

A study of the functions of state government as opposed to those of local government would in early times show that the care and maintenance of roads was primarily a local function. Gradually the need of state administration for efficient motor vehicle taxation was recognized, and more recently, as the state has assumed some of the roadbuilding functions, the growing need of state revenue for highways has added the motor transportation taxes to the list of state-administered taxes.

Professor Porter states the underlying problems in these words:

> It should not be that the people of a sparsely settled township can leave that portion of a main highway running through their jurisdiction in such condition that it is impassable, while large populations on each side of them are demanding a means of quick and easy communication.
>
> On the other hand, it is not proper that people of a sparsely settled township should be obliged to go to the expense of building a fine highway chiefly to accommodate the city population.[1]

His particular solution is a classification of highways with the state keeping up state highways and the counties and towns taking care of the county roads. Whether or not the

[1] Porter, *op. cit.*, pp. 279-80.

cost of highways has been divided according to this principle, local expenditures have developed in most instances beyond the local districts' ordinary resources.

Poll and property taxes may be, and often are, used as a local means of raising road revenue,[1] but the obvious benefit to motor vehicle owners from highway expenditure has made the state taxation of motor vehicles for road purposes peculiarly acceptable.

The problems of the motor vehicle are essentially twentieth century problems. At first it was a problem of policing or regulating only, and the earliest legislation was merely for registration of motor vehicles. New York passed the first law in 1901, and in 1903 several industrial states followed. Professor Martin shows the gradual change in the laws from fees to taxes.

The revenue idea was almost entirely missing from all the earliest legislation. In most cases, it is true, fees were charged; but they were barely sufficient to cover the cost of administering the regulatory measures.

After 1909, however, even the original laws, as they were passed in those states which still lacked them, began to show clear, though slowly developing, evidence that legislatures were becoming conscious of the possibility of making licensing of motor cars the occasion for collecting revenue. Growth of the revenue idea is apparent from the increase in the average rates, from the tendency to make the licenses annual rather than permanent, and indirectly from the attempt to secure a just distribution, evidenced by the gradation of the tax on a basis of horse power.[2]

[1] There is one road tax on property in Arizona which has become a "state-administered locally-shared tax." The rest of the road taxes and the poll taxes have remained local taxes, although they are often state controlled.

[2] Martin, "The Motor Vehicle Registration License," *National Tax Association Bulletin*, vol. xii, no. 7, April, 1927, pp. 194-5.

In many instances the motor vehicles have been exempted from the property tax and taxed by the license alone at a sufficient rate to make it an acceptable substitute for property taxation. Furthermore, the motor vehicle offered a means of reaching the special benefits in the use of the roads, so a heavier tax than on other property, or an additional tax, was considered just. For the additional tax a method was sought which would reach all motor vehicles and at the same time be acceptable from the point of view of justice. The numerous bases tried and the yearly changes in state laws are evidence of the difficulty of finding a satisfactory tax. (See Appendix 1). The New York State Special Tax Commission of 1922 writes, "The process of motorization has proceeded more rapidly than the theory of taxation in this field, and the practise of motor vehicle taxation has run beyond the technical knowledge necessary to the formulation of a form of tax which would be scientific and generally acceptable."[1] The theory which the Committee used to justify a motor vehicle tax was that road-users should pay for the highways, just as they have for the toll roads. That is to say, they justified the tax on the benefit theory.

The states have used different theories of taxation in working out motor vehicle taxation. This accounts, at least in part, for the different methods which have been evolved. Some have felt that roads, inasmuch as they add to all welfare, should be paid for by general taxation, and that although the motor vehicle may be classified in a special way, it should be taxed on value as other property is. The opposing theory used by enthusiasts for heavy motor fees is that the road-users benefit to such an extent that they should pay all costs (construction and maintenance) in a benefit or license tax based on benefit for use, or damage to the roads.

[1] New York State Special Joint Committee on Taxation and Retrenchment, *op. cit.*, p. 130.

Professor Bullock, in his comments on the report of the National Tax Association Committee on Taxation of Motor Vehicles, spoke of the evolution of taxation of motor vehicles in Massachusetts.

> A generation ago, when our states undertook to improve their highways, and a well-designed and constructed macadam road was the last word in highway transportation, it required in the State of Massachusetts something like six or seven thousand dollars a mile to build a state highroad of the best description. Then came along the motor car, which just removed the surface of those state highways and blew it into the faces of passersby, and pretty soon we were experimenting with improved surfaces and spending, say, $12,000 a mile, just because the motor car had come along. Then we looked around and said "These people are making us spend a lot of money that we would otherwise not have to spend," and we began increasing our registration fee, so as to make that pay a part, at least, of the damage done to our highways and a part of the burden that would otherwise have been forced wholly upon property owners, many of whom did not own motor cars and didn't use the highways that way. We adopted definitely the benefit principle of taxation, making people pay for what they got, which was their right—for stripping off the surface of our improved macadam roads and blowing it in everybody's face.[1]

Still other states take a middle view, and would have construction costs paid by the whole body politic and a license tax based on benefit which should be sufficient to pay upkeep. These different conceptions of the motor vehicle tax led to many different types of base for taxation. In reaching the motor vehicle as property, valuation has usually been cost price or manufacturer's list price.

According to Professor Martin the motor transportation

[1] Bullock, "Comments on a paper on Commercial Motor Transportation," *National Tax Association Proceedings*, vol. xxii, 1929, p. 521.

taxes can be reduced in general to four criteria which measure the cost of or the benefit derived from the use of the roads. These are, (1) number of miles the vehicle will be operated; (2) speed at which it will be operated; (3) gross weight of the vehicle; and (4) type of tire equipment. In order to reach the first two of these measures a tax on gasoline is commonly resorted to.[1] The motor vehicle license tax can be devised so as to combine several of the criteria. North Dakota uses as the base for motor trucks net weight, value, horsepower and capacity.

As the theory and practice of motor vehicle transportation developed it became evident that the states must do the larger share of the taxing. Also, the states were laying out tremendous sums on roads, part of which they felt should come into their coffers through the taxation of motor vehicles. So, although originally the control and building of roads, as well as the functions of collecting the taxes for roads, were local functions, the complexity of reaching the beneficiaries made it necessary for the state to administer the tax. But the cost of road upkeep has also increased for cities and other local units, so the question now is, how far should the state go in taking over the function of controlling and building the roads? Should the money be collected by the state and returned as a whole to the local districts, or should it all be retained by the state?

[1] Martin, "Some General Principles of Motor Vehicle Taxation," *National Tax Association Bulletin*, vol. xv, no. 7, April, 1930, p. 197.

TABLE VI

PRESENT STATUS OF STATE-ADMINISTERED LOCALLY-SHARED MOTOR VEHICLE AND COMMON CARRIER TAX LAWS, 1929

State	Law first dividing revenue	Jurisdiction administering	Designated use	Percentage to local district	Basis of distribution
Alabama	Motor vehicle 1911	County supervised by State	Construction of roads and payment of road bonds	20 to cities and counties	Incorporated city or town or to county if owner lives in unincorporated place
California	Motor vehicle 1913	Department of Motor Vehicles	County roads and bridges	35 to counties	Where collected
	Common carriers 1923	Department of Motor Vehicles	County roads and bridges	35 to counties	Proportion of of motor vehicles registered in each county
Colorado	Motor vehicles 1913	Secretary of State	County roads	50 to counties	Where collected
	Common carriers 1927	Public Utility Commission	Maintenance and repair of public highways in counties	45 to counties	Mileage of state routes and highways as established by state highway department
Connecticut	Common carriers 1927	State Board of Equalization	..	1 cent per mile for each mile traveled in city, county or town on roads other than state aid and trunk roads	Apportioned according to the highway used in each jurisdiction
Florida	Motor vehicle 1911	State Treasurer	County roads	25 to counties	Where collected
	Common carriers 1929	Railroad Commission	County road bonds	95 to counties	Proportion miles traveled in each county to total miles traveled
Idaho	Motor vehicles 1913	County supervised by Department of Law Enforcement	Interest and sinking fund for road bonds and roads and bridges	90 to counties[a]	Where collected

[a] Divided again.

TABLE VI—*Continued*

State	Law first dividing revenue	Jurisdiction administering	Designated use	Percentage to local district	Basis of distribution
Iowa	Motor vehicles 1911	County supervised by State	County motor vehicle fund	94 to counties	Proportion area of county to area of state
	Common carriers 1923	Railroad Commission	Roads used by common carrier	80 to cities and counties	Proportion of city and county roads to roads used
Kansas	Common carriers 1925	County supervised by State	..	80 to counties[a]	Proportion of miles of road in counties and cities
Kentucky	Motor vehicles 1924	State Tax Commission	..	50 to counties	Divided equally
Maryland	Motor vehicles 1916	Commissioner of Motor Vehicles	Streets and roads	20 to Baltimore	
	Common carriers 1916	Public Service Commission	Roads	100 to counties, cities and towns	In proportion to miles of road used in each
Michigan	Motor vehicle 1915	Secretary of State	Construction and maintenance of roads	Six million dollars to counties[a]	Proportioned to fees from each county
Mississippi	Motor vehicle 1922	County supervised by State	Roads, bridges and culverts	100 to counties	Where collected
Montana	Motor vehicle 1917	Secretary of State	County road funds	100 to counties	Where collected
Nebraska	Motor vehicle 1911	County supervised by State	Road dragging funds	70 to counties	Where collected
Nevada	Common carriers 1925	Public Service Commission	County road fund	100 to counties	Proportioned to route used in county
New Mexico	Motor vehicle 1923	Registrar	17 per cent county road fund. 25 per cent schools	42 to counties[a]	Proportioned to motor vehicle registration

[a] Divided again.

TABLE VI—*Continued*

State	Law first dividing revenue	Jurisdiction administering	Designated use	Percentage to local district	Basis of distribution
New York	Motor vehicle 1916	Secretary of State	County and town roads supervised by state highway commissioner	25 to counties[a]	Where collected
North Dakota	Motor vehicle 1911	Registrar	County road fund	50 per cent over $280,000 to counties	Where collected
Ohio	Motor vehicle 1919	State Treasurer	Roads	50 to cities or counties	Number of motor vehicles in area
	Common carriers 1923	State Treasurer	Roads	50 to cities and counties	Proportioned to miles of route traveled in each
Oklahoma	Motor vehicle 1915	Department of Highways	Construction and maintenance of roads	60 to counties[a]	Proportioned to amount collected
Oregon	Motor vehicle 1913	Secretary of State	Interest on bonds, preparing highway, or as county court decrees	33⅓ to counties	Where collected
	Common carriers 1925	Public Service Commission	Interest on bonds, preparing highway, or as county court decrees	25 to counties	Proportioned to motor vehicle licenses
South Carolina	Common carriers 1925	Road Commissioner	Roads	100, all collected for use of county, city and town highways	Proportioned to miles of route on each
South Dakota	Motor vehicle 1913	County supervised by State	Grading, crossing, etc.	48 to counties	Where collected
Tennessee	Motor vehicle 1919	County supervised by State	State highway commissioner may designate roads	50 to counties	Divided equally

[a] Divided again.

TABLE VI—*Concluded*

State	Law first dividing revenue	Jurisdiction administering	Designated use	Percentage to local district	Basis of distribution
Texas	Motor vehicle 1917	County supervised by State	Roads supervised by county engineer	17½ cents per horse power taxed plus 30 per cent weight fees to counties	Where collected
	Common carriers 1918	State Highway Department	County roads	100 up to $50,000; 50 up to $75,000	Where collected
Virginia	Common carriers 1923	Tax Commissioner	Roads	100 to counties	Proportion of county roads to total roads used
Washington	Motor vehicle 1915	County supervised by State	Roads	100 counties[a]	County where collected

[a] Divided again.

Before deciding what should be done it is well to find out how far the state legislation has developed. All forty-eight states have special motor vehicle taxes, so that although in some cities there are local licenses in addition to the state licenses, for the most part the locality can only tax the motor vehicles as personal property, if at all. The amount obtained in this way for both state and local property taxes is such a small proportion of the total amount collected from all forms of motor transportation taxation (in 1929 $140,000,000 out of $925,000,000) [1] that it is necessary for the state to share its licenses with the locality if the local district is to retain much of the road-building function.

Of the forty-eight states having state license taxes,

[1] "Special Taxation for Motor Vehicles, 1930," *National Automobile Chamber of Commerce*, Washington, 1930, p. 3.

twenty-two share the revenue in whole or in part with the local districts. In some cases the tax is collected for the state by the locality, the state furnishing the license plates and auditing the accounts. These have been included as state-administered taxes, as they cannot be evaded even if the locality is lax in its tax administration. Of the twenty-six state laws not included in this study, seven have specific provisions in the law that the money is to be used partially for county roads, lateral roads, or county aid, but the revenue is either spent by an officer of state government or loses its identity in being returned as part of a local subsidy which is derived from many sources.

The principle of sharing the revenue from the tax is found first in 1911 when Alabama, Florida, Iowa, Nebraska and North Dakota all started it. The majority of such laws were introduced in the decade 1910-1920. The latest state to introduce sharing was Kentucky in 1924.[1] The local share has been withdrawn in certain instances. Arkansas, for instance, divided the tax in 1913, but in 1929 turned all the revenue into the state highway fund for administration.

To answer the question of whether or not the locality should share the tax requires an inquiry as to why the states which share the revenue do so. In the states which no longer assess the motor vehicle for the state personal property tax, seven make no return to the localities; in the other six the proportion returned varies from ninety per cent in Idaho to twenty-five per cent in New York State. The variation makes it impossible to say that exemption from the personal property tax means any definite state policy as to returning revenue except that the state in no case returns all of the revenue. Eighteen of the states return the revenue where collected, so it seems in the majority of cases to be an example of sharing a source of taxation to which the state

[1] *Cf. supra*, p. 37.

feels that both state and local district have a claim. Two states, Kentucky and Tennessee, divide the local share equally among the counties, giving each county the same flat amount. By this distribution the poorer counties are aided by the wealthier counties. The other two states return the local shares by different methods, each of which is an attempt to get at the needs of the locality. Maryland gives twenty per cent to Baltimore for city pavements; Iowa returns it in proportion to the area of the county.

A definite trend toward state control of this function is seen in the history of the proportion of the tax which is returned. Although six states have increased the proportion, six have kept it the same, and in nine states the proportion has been reduced. Texas has changed from a percentage return to a flat amount plus a smaller percentage, which at present gives the local districts a larger proportion of the tax than they had before. The reduction of the percentage to go to the locality does not necessarily mean a smaller amount of money, but it often means that the states are assuming a larger proportion of the road expense. The present proportions returned to the states may be divided into three groups, (1) those returning one hundred per cent; (2) those returning more than fifty per cent and less than one hundred per cent; and (3) those returning less than fifty per cent. The three states returning one hundred per cent, Washington, Mississippi and Montana, formerly returned less. Of the nine states in the second group only Idaho and Iowa have increased the proportion returned; three, Colorado, Kentucky and Ohio, have not changed the proportion; four, Nebraska, North Dakota, Oklahoma and Tennessee have reduced the proportion returned. In the last group there are eight states, three of which, California, Maryland and New Mexico have not changed the proportion returned, but five of these, Alabama, Florida, New York, Oregon and South

Dakota, have decreased the relative amount returned. Michigan and Texas have changed from a percentage return to a flat amount. There has been a tendency as the motor vehicle taxes become established to decrease the proportion going back.

The actual amount of money received by the local districts from motor vehicles and common carriers has, however, been growing rapidly. It has increased from $905,000 in 1912 to $58,246,000 in 1925 and $67,020,000 in 1928. The proportion received from the motor vehicle compared to the total local tax revenue from state-administered locally-shared taxes has also increased from 5.7 per cent in 1912 to 31.2 per cent in 1925 and 25.7 per cent in 1928. The increase in the amount is the result of an increase in the rates of the license tax, an increase in the number of automobiles, as well as an increase in the number of states levying the tax. In spite of the fact that the proportion returned to the localities is less, the actual amount is greater. The proportion of revenues which has been returned with special directions for spending it is also greater, so that it can still be said that state control within the field of motor vehicle taxation is growing.

Only one state, Kentucky, returns the tax without any requirement governing the spending of it. However, the requirements of the others that the money be spent for the maintenance and construction of roads may not have any important effect on county financing, as the county can use this money for roads, and thus have free whatever revenue it collects itself for other purposes. It will be only in case the revenue returned for roads is out of proportion to the rest of the county expenditures, or if the requirements to be fulfilled are too numerous, that the county will be hampered. There does seem to be some tendency to increase requirements, as the Alabama, California, Florida, Oregon and

South Dakota laws, which at first had no specifications, now require that the revenue be used for roads only. New York and Tennessee not only require that the money be spent for roads, but they also demand that the state supervise the building of the roads. In Tennessee the state may require the county to match the revenue returned. Since 1924 California has required that the road work done with these funds be reported to the state department of public works. So regulation has increased, and although it may not seriously hamper the counties in the performance of this function, the indications are that the state is tending to take over the road building function. That this is what is happening is indicated again by the fact that six state taxes which were once divided are now entirely state-administered and expended. Arkansas, Georgia, Kansas, North Carolina, South Carolina and Wisconsin are returning the whole revenue to state highway commissions to administer. It is often on county roads that the money is spent, but it is without any county control. All of the states are spending vastly larger sums on roads than formerly.

COMMON CARRIER TAXES

The rapid development of motor trucks and buses as a means of commercial transportation has brought problems different from those of the motor vehicle as an instrument for the conveyance of the person or property of the owner of the vehicle. As soon as a charge is made for transportation the service becomes vested with public interest.[1] The motor buses come into competition with the railroads which pay for their roadbeds, and it is unfair competition unless the motor buses pay a special tax for the use of the roads. The public becomes interested also from the point of view of service and charge made for public transportation. There are thirty-

[1] Hunter, "The Taxation of Commercial Motor Transportation," *National Tax Association Proceedings*, vol. xxi, 1928, p. 182.

one states where the common carriers are given special consideration apart from the motor vehicles. In the preamble of the act for the taxation of common carriers in Nevada there is mentioned the benefit received by the user, and in addition the valuable franchise, as the reasons for a special franchise tax.

Whereas the operation of motor trucks and motor vehicles, at frequent intervals, over the roads and improved highways of this state, is known to rapidly destroy the said roads and improved highways so as to increase the cost of maintenance of said roads and highways, and in many instances to introduce elements of danger to the traveling public; and Whereas it is necessary for the enforcement of good order and for the protection of roads and highways constructed by this state and the counties thereof, that the state spend large sums of money for the regulation and supervision of such roads and highways, and for the repairs to damages done to said roads and highways; and, Whereas, a valuable franchise is given to every person, association or corporation who is permitted to use the highways of this state for the transportation of property or persons for hire in any established common carrier, truck, or passenger line, which may be given a certificate of public convenience and necessity under the laws of this state; and, Whereas, this act is necessary for the preservation of public safety and the support of existing institutions of the State of Nevada, the people of Nevada, represented by the Senate and Assembly, pass a franchise tax on such companies.[1]

The two principles, then, upon which the special common carrier tax is levied are, first, for benefit in the use of the roads, and secondly, as a business carried on for profit in which the state furnishes the highways as a vital part of the business equipment.

By definition a common carrier would not include buses

[1] *Nevada Statutes*, 1925, ch. 162, p. 247.

running between fixed termini which do business for one or two establishments; but in so far as the use of the roads and the franchise given are practically the same, and very few such buses are not common carriers, many laws do not distinguish between them.[1] Professor Bullock, in discussing the justification of the tax for commercial motor trucks, includes all buses, whether common carriers or not.

In the first place these perfectly good macadam roads, with a hard surface that was sufficient to stand the suction of the tires on the rapidly moving motor cars, were knocked into bits, and we had to reconstruct our roads again. [The roads for the motor car] did not provide the sub-structure and the wider roadway needed for these enormous motor trucks and motor buses, with the result that we applied the benefit principle further and increased our taxes all along the line, though we had some difficulties in dealing with the new class of transportation agencies. . . . Until we put upon these new agencies a tax that makes them pay a proper charge for the improved highways, they force us to construct at public expense for their parasitic industries; we don't know what the cost of transportation is; we don't know whether they are giving the public a cheaper form of transportation, to which the public is entitled; or whether they are giving a more expensive form of transportation, the cost of which is camouflaged by giving them a subsidy and ground toll, in the form of a $60,000 highway to operate on and then covering it up in the general tax levy on property.[2]

There are seventeen states which treat the common carrier as other motor vehicles. The taxes in seven of these, New York, Idaho, Kentucky, Tennessee, Mississippi, New Mexico and Washington, are among the taxes already discussed at state-administered locally-shared motor vehicle taxes. In

[1] Hunter, *op. cit.*, pp. 201-2.

[2] Bullock, *op. cit.*, pp. 521-2.

the other ten states neither the motor vehicle nor the common carrier taxes are divided. There are thirty-one states which tax the common carrier separately, and of these thirteen have a tax which is state-administered and locally-shared. This makes twenty laws by which common carrier taxes are divided. The present discussion will treat only of the thirteen where the taxes are separated, as the others have already been discussed.

In the thirteen cases where the common carriers are treated separately they always pay in addition the gasoline tax, and eight pay the regular tax on motor vehicles. The reason for this is not apparent in the taxes, as they have no distinguishing features, but vary, as do the additional common carrier taxes, in bases for taxation, amounts returned and dates of passage.

These thirteen laws are of comparatively recent date, the oldest being the Maryland law of 1916, and nearly all of them are as recent as 1923 or later. They correspond to the development of the commercial freight and passenger carrier which has gone forward rapidly since the war. The basis of the tax in most cases is some measure which attempts to put a franchise tax on the earnings of the common carrier, the basis being income, the miles traveled, carrying capacity, weight or earnings.

The local share of the tax is returned in recognition of the privilege of using county and city highways. This is clearly indicated by the bases used for distribution.

In giving revenue to the local districts, ten states make the percentage definite. Three, South Carolina, Virginia and Maryland, follow the benefit theory by dividing the revenue between the state and the counties according to the proportion of state and county highways over which the bus travels. Of those returning a definite proportion, one, Nevada, returns one hundred per cent; five, Florida, Iowa, Kansas,

Ohio and Texas, give back from ninety-nine to fifty per cent; and California, Colorado, Connecticut and Oregon give less than fifty per cent. In general it can be said that the tax is one which is in large part returned to the local district.

The tax is returned largely on the basis of mileage traveled on county or city highways. Nine states, Connecticut, Florida, Iowa, Kansas, Maryland, Nevada, Ohio, South Carolina and Virginia all use this method. This is reapportionment of the tax, as the business is taxed at its main office, and the money is returned according to benefit derived by prorating it on a mileage basis. California and Oregon reapportion the tax, on the basis of the proportion of motor vehicles registered in each county as compared to the total number in the state, and Colorado and Texas do not reapportion it but return it to the counties where it was collected. In come cases, as in Kansas, the county is required to redivide the revenue among cities and towns, and sometimes, for example in the case of the Maryland tax, the state itself makes all the division.

The purpose for which the tax is returned might well be expected to be for roads, and nine of the states do make specific requirements that it be used for roads or for the county road fund. Two have other specific uses designated. Florida and Oregon require that it be used to pay bonds issued for road building, and if any revenue remains it is to be used for roads. However, the effect of this large proportion for roads, as has been said before, depends on the amount of revenue returned in proportion to other local revenue. On the whole it would seem that there is a decided tendency to reapportion the revenue of common carrier taxes, in common with other motor vehicle taxes, and to specify the way in which it shall be used.

GASOLINE TAXES

The second general type of motor transportation tax is the gasoline tax.

The Special Joint Committee on Taxation and Retrenchment of New York in 1922, in recommending the gasoline tax, said

The Committee recommends that a tax on gasoline be made a part of the system of taxes on motor transportation. . . . The gasoline tax makes possible a fairer distribution of the motor traffic taxes than would be possible with vehicle fees alone. It appears to be the best practicable measure of the use of the roads. It makes it possible to take mileage into account in apportioning the cost of the roads, and it reaches the cars of other states operating in New York.[1]

The gasoline tax is quite universally justified on the benefit theory. The following preamble to the Nevada law of 1923 shows evidence of this:

Whereas—gasoline, distillate and other volatile and inflamable liquids are used extensively to operate and propel motor vehicles, machines, and engines over and upon the roads and highways of the State of Nevada; and Whereas—the operation of said motor vehicles, machines, and engines over and upon the roads and highways of this state by means of the use of said gasoline, distillate and other volatile and inflammable liquids produced for the purpose of operating or propelling motor vehicles is destructive of said roads and highways; and Whereas—the successful operation of such vehicles, machines and engines over public roads and highways of this state depends to a large extent upon construction and maintenance of good roads, which are exceedingly expensive; Whereas—the state and the various counties within the state have expended large sums of public money for the construction of expensive roads and high-

[1] "Special Joint Committee on Taxation and Retrenchment," *op. cit.*, p. 151.

ways which are of an immense benefit to the persons operating said vehicles, machines and engines; and Whereas—the movement of said vehicles over the highways of the state is attended by constant and serious danger to the public; and Whereas—it is necessary for the enforcement of good order, as well as upkeep of the public roads and highways constructed by this state and the various counties thereof, that the state expend large sums of money for the regulation and supervising of such vehicles, machines and engines upon the public highway, and for the repair of the damage done to said highway: therefore,—The People of the State of Nevada, represented by the Senate and Assembly, do enact as follows:—an excise tax on gasoline.[1]

In discussing the justification for the gasoline tax Professor Hunter says: " The justification for the use of gasoline as a base for tax levy does not necessarily depend upon the expenditure of receipts for highway purposes." [2] He cites as examples Florida, Georgia and South Dakota, which states use part of the revenue of the gasoline tax for schools:

Any justification for such use of receipts from the gasoline tax must be upon some other basis than the benefit received from the expenditure of the funds. If the principle be accepted that taxes should be levied on the basis of ability to pay, and it can be shown that taxes upon gasoline conform to this, then there is justification for a levy greater or less than that sufficient to finance highways.[3]

The fact that the gasoline tax is used to only a limited extent for other than highway expenditure would argue that the benefit theory is by far the more important. Cities and towns claim a share on the ground that their local highway

[1] *Nevada Statutes*, 1923, ch. 180, p. 317.

[2] " Report of the Committee on Taxation of Commercial Motor Vehicle Transportation," *National Tax Association Proceedings*, vol. xxii, 1929, p. 472.

[3] *Ibid.*, p. 473.

expenditures benefit the motor vehicle owners. Undoubtedly it is also because of the local need and high road standards set by the state government that so many states feel compelled to share this form of taxation.

A survey of the proportions returned to the localities indicates that the states are using the gasoline tax more and more as a source of state revenue, for although they usually return the same flat amount per gallon of gasoline taxed, they do not usually share the revenue from any new or increased taxes on gasoline. Alabama is the only state returning one hundred per cent of the tax, although in the first year, 1923, it divided the tax, it returned only fifty per cent. Mississippi, Arizona and Florida return fifty per cent of the tax and eighteen states return less than fifty per cent. None of these has increased the proportion of the tax returned, but rather, ten of the states have decreased the proportion returned, usually by increasing the tax levy and keeping all of the extra levy for the state. More and more the gasoline tax is going wholly to state treasuries, just as the motor vehicle tax is.

The total amount which is shared is $64,237,000, or 24.6 per cent of all locally-shared taxes. As with the motor vehicle tax which is shared, the amount is increasing. The proportion that this share is of the total local revenue is also increasing, but it is a decreasing proportion of the total revenue received from the gasoline tax.

Taxation of gasoline as part of the state revenue system is a new tax, the first laws having been passed in 1919 by Colorado, New Mexico, North Dakota and Oregon. Of the forty-eight states having gasoline taxes, twenty-four return all or part of the tax.

TABLE VII

PRESENT STATUS OF STATE-ADMINISTERED LOCALLY-SHARED GASOLINE TAX LAWS, 1929

State	Law first dividing revenue	Jurisdiction administering	Designated use	Percentage to local district	Basis of distribution
Alabama	1923	State Tax Commission	Construction and maintenance roads and bridges	100 to counties	Divided equally
Arizona	1923	Motor Vehicle Department	Maintenance roads and bridges	37½ to counties, 12½ to cities and towns	Where collected
California	1923	State Comptroller	Construction and maintenance roads and bridges	33⅓ to counties	In proportion to motor vehicles registered
Colorado	1919	State Oil Inspector	Construction and maintenance of roads	27 to counties	In proportion to mileage of state highway
Florida	1923	State Comptroller	Schools, construction of roads. Pay road bonds	22$\frac{2}{9}$ to counties 44$\frac{4}{9}$ to counties	Divided equally Where collected
Georgia	1923	Comptroller General	Construction and maintenance roads and bridges	16⅔ to counties	Proportioned to miles of state aid system of roads in each county
Illinois	1927	Department of Finance	Construction of state aid roads	33⅓ to counties	Proportioned to motor vehicle licenses in each county
Indiana	1923	State Auditor	¾ for special county road fund. ¼ city streets	25 to counties, cities and towns and villages	¾ to counties one-half according miles free gravel roads in county in proportion to state and one-half equally. ¼ to cities, towns and villages according population compared to state

TABLE VII—*Continued*

State	Law first dividing revenue	Jurisdiction administering	Designated use	Percentage to local district	Basis of distribution
Iowa	1925	State Treasurer	..	22⅜ to counties 22⅜ to towns	Proportion area county bears state area Proportion town roads bears to county roads
Kansas	1927	State Oil Inspector	Roads	$3,600,000 to counties[a]	40 per cent divided equally. 60 per cent by assessed valuation
Mary-land	1927	State Treasurer	Eliminate grade crossings	2½ to Baltimore	
Michigan	1927	Secretary of State	Roads	Counties, difference between six million dollars and 50 per cent of weight tax on motor vehicles[a]	⅞ in proportion to weight tax; ⅛ divided equally
Mis-sissippi	1922	Auditor of Public Accounts	Construction and maintenance of roads	60 to counties	In proportion to number registered motor vehicles
Ne-braska	1929	State Treasurer	Roads	25 to counties	In proportion to number of registered motor vehicles
New York	1929	Department of Taxation and Finance	In New York City to reduce taxes; counties for highways	20 to New York City; 5 to counties	Proportion public highway in counties outside cities bears to total public highway in state outside cities

[a] Divided again.

TABLE VII—*Continued*

State	Law first dividing revenue	Jurisdiction administering	Designated use	Percentage to local district	Basis of distribution
North Carolina	1929	State Treasurer	Road fund to reduce road tax	20 to counties	½ according proportion area of county bears state area. ½ according proportion population in 1920 of county bears state population
North Dakota	1929	State Auditor	County roads	33⅓ to counties	Proportion registration motor vehicles
Ohio	1925	State Tax Commission	Counties, widening roads;	5 to counties	Equally divided
			towns, improving roads;	10 to towns	Equally divided
			cities, city streets	5 to cities	Number registered motor vehicles
Oklahoma	1923	Oil Inspector	Roads and bridges	25 to counties	Proportion population, valuation, and area of county bear to state
Pennsylvania	1921	Department of Revenue	Construction and maintenance roads	12½ to counties	Where collected
South Carolina	1922	State Tax Commission	Construction and maintenance roads	16⅔ to counties	Proportion of motor vehicle fees collected
Virginia	1923	Motor Vehicle Commission	County highway system, county must match ⅓ of the money	33⅓ to counties	As state aid is apportioned [b]

[b] State aid apportioned according to the amount of state taxes paid to the Treasurer from the County on real estate, personal property, income, and capitation taxes the next preceding fiscal year.

TABLE VII—*Concluded*

State	Law first dividing revenue	Jurisdiction administering	Designated use	Percentage to local district	Basis of distribution
Washington	1929	State Treasurer	Improve lateral roads	33⅓ to counties[a]	½ divided equally, ¼ in proportion number registered motor vehicles, ¼ in proportion number of farms
Wyoming	1929	State Treasurer	Road fund	25 to counties	30 per cent by area; 30 per cent by population; 40 per cent by assessed valuation, county to state

[a] Divided again.

The bases used are so widely diversified that no one can be designated as predominant. There are, in all, nine different methods used, and many states use two or three of them. One method is to divide the revenue equally among the counties giving each county the same flat amount. This method is used for all of the Alabama returns, for fifty per cent of the Florida returns, for forty per cent of the Kansas returns, twelve and one-half per cent of the Michigan returns, seventy-five per cent of the Ohio returns, and fifty per cent of the Washington returns. Two states, Arizona and Pennsylvania, used the second method, returning the tax to the localities, where it is collected. Florida uses this method for distribution of half of the revenue shared. The third method is to return it in proportion to the number of motor vehicles registered in each locality. This method is used by California, Illinois, Mississippi, Nebraska, North Dakota, South Carolina, twenty-five per cent of the Ohio tax, twenty-five per cent of the Virginia tax, eighty-seven and one-half per cent of the Michigan tax and twenty-five per cent of the Washington tax. This would seem to be an attempt to return the tax to the place where the largest part of the traffic is centered, and therefore where highway needs are great. The fourth method is to distribute the tax according to the proportion of public highways in each county, and is used by Colorado, Georgia and Indiana (34 per cent), Iowa (50 per cent) and New York (20 per cent). This is another way of trying to get at the same thing that the third method accomplishes, that is, to distribute to the municipalities approximately in proportion to highway needs. The fifth method is distribution according to population, and is used by Indiana (25 per cent), North Carolina (50 per cent), Oklahoma (33⅓ per cent) and Wyoming (30 per cent). The sixth method is to return the revenue according to the area of the county in comparison with the total area of the state, and is used by Iowa (50 per cent), North Carolina (50 per cent), Oklahoma (33⅓ per cent) and Wyoming (30 per cent). These last two methods are further attempts to divide according to need, but they would seem to be poorer bases for measuring such need. The seventh method is according to the assessed valuation of the locality, and is used by Kansas (60 per cent), Oklahoma (33⅓ per cent) and Wyoming (40 per cent). Virginia is the only state using the eighth method, which is a division according to the amount of state property tax received, from each county. This would presumably have much the same results as the preceding method. A very interesting method, especially in view of the present agricultural situation, is that used by Washington. Twenty-five per cent of the revenue is divided according to the number of farms.

The requirements made as conditions to the return of the gasoline tax are almost universally the same, *i.e.*, that it shall be used for roads, bridges and culverts. Iowa, it is true, makes no requirement, and Florida requires a portion of it to be used for schools. However, twenty-one of the twenty-three states designating the use to be made of the revenue return it with the general requirement that it be used for roads and bridges and seven states, Indiana, Kansas, Maryland, Michigan, New York, Ohio and Washington, are required to give some part of it to the cities or towns for city streets and town roads. Although undoubtedly the cities share in the portion of the counties in other instances, this is not a state requirement. North Carolina specifies that the county use the tax to reduce the ad valorem tax for roads. This, plus the money from motor vehicles which is returned for a designated use, makes a large amount for required local use and raises the question of desirability of so much control. This will be discussed in connection with motor transportation taxes in general in a later section.

Generally speaking, the money is returned to the county in such a way as to have considerable effect on county expenditures. In the first place, all but one tax reapportions the money according to some principle or theory which the state wishes to stress. In the second place, it is returned, on the whole, for specific purposes. The purpose of this last may be that the state tends to recognize from experience that money returned to the county is best returned with restrictions. Since the gasoline tax is so new it would show the result of this experience; or it may be that the gasoline tax is the type of tax which really belongs to the state, since it is not in any way part of the old property tax, as the motor vehicle excise is, and the money shared is more like a subvention, and therefore subject to requirements. Whatever the reason, there is considerable state control of the counties through the revenue returned from the gasoline tax.

It is perhaps significant that there are three gasoline taxes which were originally shared taxes and have since become wholly state taxes. This probably means that certain expenditures which were formerly controlled by the local districts have now become direct state expenditures. The Arkansas tax which was divided in 1921 was at first shared with the county where it was collected. The amount shared was first increased and then decreased, and in 1927 only enough was left to pay county bonds; then in 1929 the yield of the tax was put entirely under the control of the state highway department. The Nevada law has had much the same history, although it was not divided until 1923. The same is also true of the Montana law, divided first in 1921. This first sharing of revenue was for school purposes, but was changed two years later to road funds for the county, and in 1927 the whole tax was turned over to the state highway fund to be administered by the state highway commission.

All of these indications seem to point to a decided tendency to use the sharing of revenue as an intermediate step toward full state control, or a fully protected subsidy by the state, for road construction and maintenance.

GENERAL CONCLUSIONS ON MOTOR TRANSPORTATION TAXES

As the figures of the amount given back from common carrier taxes are usually combined with those from all motor vehicles, the amount returned and reapportioned must be discussed together. Since the three motor transportation taxes are so closely allied in effect it seemed well to consider the combined effect of these taxes on local finances. The total amount of revenue returned from all of these taxes was $131,257,000 in 1928. Of this revenue $127,500,000 was returned with the purpose designated, $980,000 to be used for schools, and $126,520,000 to be used for roads. In other words, 99.2 per cent of the revenue returned must be used by the localities for roads. This is 19.2 per cent of the total amount of tax revenue devoted to local road expenditure, which means that the localities are raising a large percentage of the road revenues from their own taxes. But to carry on the extensive improvements demanded today, they need the nineteen per cent supplied by the states.

Considering that it is only nineteen per cent of all of the money which the localities spend for roads, it is not possible to say that the amount returned is excessive in comparison with all taxes spent for roads. The state is not, probably, forcing the local districts to spend more than they would otherwise spend, nor is the state forcing the local district to divert money from other uses, as the states do not require the locality to match the money or come up to minimum standards. It is, however, considerable control when the state is to a large extent controlling nineteen per cent of the local expenditures or revenues. The state spends from its own tax revenue $560,335,000 per year on highways, bridges and culverts, and adding to it $126,520,000 which the state dictates that the counties shall use for the purpose of roads it makes a total of $686,875,000 which the state controls out of the $1,245,440,000 of tax revenues spent by state and local units.[1] The state, then, has taken on the direction of half of the taxes expended for roads.

There is a definite trend toward full retention by the state of the taxes now divided. In the case of motor vehicles there are six state laws which once used the state-administered locally-shared tax method and now retain the full yield. In addition three gasoline taxes have already passed through this evolution, although the gasoline tax is a comparatively new tax. These nine examples show that in motor transportation state-administered locally-shared taxes

[1] Figures for state and local expenditures from the United States Department of Agriculture, *Bureau of Public Roads*, 1928.

are a transitional step toward full state control of the revenue, and with it the building of roads.

Since there is no doubt that the states are gradually taking more and more of the road-building function into their hands, in concluding a discussion of motor transportation it seems well to consider again whether or not the road-building function is a local one. Professor Martin makes a very strong plea for entirely state-controlled roads, on the ground that this is the more efficient method. He says "where funds are now distributed wholly or in part to localities it is usually a result of archaic legal restrictions, as in Kansas, or of political restraint expressing itself in the desire for local self-government." [1] He believes that we would have better results if the state highway departments did everything, as they would be more free from political influence, the state engineers would see the system as a whole, and the salaries offered might be high enough to attract trained engineers. "In any event, the most successful states in rural highway building have been those with the best organized and best developed highway departments in charge of the actual construction of the bulk of the main roads of the commonwealth." [2]

It is clear that the state is the agency for collecting taxes for roads, but after all, are there not certain benefits derived from having the local unit control local road building? Certainly many incorporated municipalities are large enough to achieve the efficiencies claimed for the state departments. A city has many streets which are of purely local concern. The motor vehicle owner benefits from these streets as well as from the state highways. Why should the cities be denied a share of state taxes on the motor vehicles, some of which (*i.e.*, delivery trucks and taxis) never go outside city limits?

[1] Martin, *op. cit.*, p. 12.

[2] *Ibid.*, p. 12.

A special problem arises in those localities where the budget is not large enough to make the adjustment to a fluctuating expenditure for roads. Take for instance the poor county which receives too little from shared taxes in any one year to carry on any extensive road-building program. The county may start a new county road which, although necessary, will be held up in building until the revenue from the state is large enough to carry it on.

The case for dividing the motor transportation taxes is stronger than that for returning other taxes, for the chief theoretical foundation for these taxes is that of benefit received. It seems to be feasible to return to the cities a proportion based upon mileage and motor vehicle registration. The rest of the taxes (*i.e.*, that not returned to the cities) should either be returned to a unit large enough to have a budget which can compensate for fluctuating needs, or else the rest of the tax should be left with the state to be used for the construction of county and town highways under state supervision. This would mean a sufficiently large sum for the state to carry through to completion in a short time a few of the most necessary county highways instead of having many counties and towns with partially finished highways. A third option is to give a subsidy which is limited to local needs and carries more definite specifications as to use than do the returns from the present state-administered locally-shared taxes each year to the counties and towns for highway building. If this is done, the subsidy must at least equal the revenue which the county or town receives now. From a practical point of view this last suggestion seems the best method of sharing the revenue with counties and towns, for, although one may argue that the state could do the work more efficiently, the American doctrine of home rule must still be remembered.

CHAPTER VI

State-Administered Locally-Shared Income Taxes

Since 1911 the personal income tax has become an important part of state tax systems in the United States. Pofessor Seligman, in discussing the development of different forms of taxation, says:

> Thus it is that in recent decades the tendency has arisen to substitute personal taxes for the older real taxes, and to assess the individual rather than the thing; or, stating it in simple language, to put revenue or income in the place of proceeds or earnings as the test of taxation. . . . From the modern point of view, it is the duty of the citizen to support the government according to his capacity to support himself.[1]

In his presidential address to the National Tax Association in 1915 Professor Seligman gave the theory of the income tax, and stated that the property tax is no longer a good state tax. "Let us recognize the fact then, once and for all, that a system of property taxation, except in so far as certain forms of real estate are concerned, is unsuited to modern economic conditions as the ordinary and principal source of revenue." [2] Classification of property may be considered a step in advance, but a makeshift justifiable for taxation of personal property only when no more radical change can be made.

The income tax was not a new tax in 1911. It had been

[1] Seligman, *op. cit.*, p. 15.

[2] Seligman, "Address," *National Tax Association Proceedings*, vol. ix, 1915, p. 134.

tried at various times under different conditions in the United States. The older income taxes have been divided by Professor Seligman in his discussion of income taxes in 1911 into four different stages of development.

First, the survival and development of the old faculty tax of colonial times; second, the partial resort to income taxes as a result of the fiscal difficulties of the early forties; third, the utilization of the income tax, especially by the southern commonwealths during the period of the Civil War; and fourth, the newer movements of the last two decades.[1]

He concludes at that time that "From the preceding survey it will be seen how utterly insignificant and unsuccessful have been the experiments with state income taxes in the United States."[2] He stated that these failures were due to poor administration. Professor Seligman pointed the way to revise the old laws and aided the movement toward the modern, successful personal income taxes.

The difficulties of the general property tax were so great and so widespread that there was a general movement toward tax reform, and many states began to consider the use of the personal income tax. The Wisconsin law of 1911 was the first to be established along more modern lines. The tax has been adopted by many other states, until today there are sixteen states which have a personal income tax. Although the Virginia law dates back to 1843, new amendments have made it really effective only recently.

There are two different types of state income taxes which Professor Leland describes in his book on the classified property tax. The first type is the general tax upon all income, regardless of the source from which it comes. The New York, North Carolina, North Dakota, Oklahoma, South

[1] Edwin R. A. Seligman, *Income Tax*, New York, 1911, p. 388.

[2] *Ibid.*, p. 418.

Carolina, Virginia and Wisconsin taxes are of this general type. The New York and Wisconsin taxes supplanted property taxes on intangibles, and the success of those taxes has led many to advocate them as a method of solving the problem of taxing intangibles. The second type of income tax is the tax designed to reach income from a specified source. Massachusetts and New Hampshire have income taxes on intangibles in lieu of the personal property tax on these sources.[1]

The fact that the income tax is in part a tax to reach the property which the localities had difficulty in reaching, but which nevertheless they considered a source of revenue, makes it seem only just that the state should return a portion of this tax. This is especially true of the income tax laws which remove intangible property from the local jurisdiction for taxation. Of the sixteen state income tax laws in the United States at present five divide the revenue with the local district. Although the number shared is small, we can discern certain tendencies in them.

The reason for returning a share of the tax becomes evident from this history of the tax. It has usually been the rule when the personal income tax is established to make the tax in lieu of the intangible property tax on individuals. This has had the effect of reducing the local tax base. The sharing of the revenue has undoubtedly been done to replace the revenue the local jurisdiction formerly got from this property.

The present proportion of the tax returned in Wisconsin, is sixty per cent of the amount collected. This has been reduced from ninety per cent, as the state decided that the amount returned was in many cases more than the local districts needed. In New York fifty per cent of the revenue is returned to the local districts. Massachusetts and New

[1] S. E. Leland, *The Classified Property Tax*, New York, 1928, p. 407.

TABLE VIII

PRESENT STATUS OF STATE-ADMINISTERED LOCALLY-SHARED PERSONAL INCOME TAX LAWS, 1929

State	Law first dividing revenue	Jurisdiction administering	Designated use	Percentage to local district	Basis of distribution
Massachusetts	1916	Commission of Corporations and Taxation	..	100 to cities and towns	In proportion to amount of state property tax assessed on cities and towns each year
New Hampshire	1923	State Tax Commission	..	100 to cities and towns, 100 to counties	Where taxpayer lives Where taxpayer lives if in unincorporated place
New York	1919	State Tax Commission	New York City to reduce taxes	50 to counties[a]	Proportion assessed value of real property of county to that of state
Tennessee	1929	Commission of Finance and Taxation	..	45 to cities, towns or counties	Where taxpayer resides
Wisconsin	1911	State Tax Commission	..	10 to counties 50 to cities, towns or villages	Where assessed, unless more than 2 per cent equalized value of city, town, or village. Such excess hall be paid to[s] cities, towns, or villages in state according to school population

[a] Divided again.

Hampshire return the full revenue, and Tennessee returns forty-five per cent. As all of these last three taxes are only on the yield of certain intangible property rather than on all personal income the yield is not as large as under the Wisconsin and New York laws.

The total amount of yield from income taxes returned to the counties in 1928 was $57,505,000 or 22.0 per cent of all state-administered locally-shared taxes.

The results of the returns have been varied. Wisconsin and New York have found certain difficulties. In New York, according to Mr. A. E. Holcomb, secretary of the National Tax Association, since there is no requirement on how the money shall be spent the results in each district are "weird and meaningless".[1] He, therefore, advocates distribution for educational purposes under the state educational department as "state aid".

Wisconsin has had difficulty because the revenue returned in some years has exceeded local needs. Professor Comstock, in her discussion of income taxes, tells how the amounts returned in some local districts were so large that the tax commission advocated lowering of the proportions returned.[2] In 1925 Wisconsin reduced the proportion returned from seventy per cent for the cities, towns and villages and twenty per cent for the county to fifty per cent for the cities, towns and villages and ten per cent for the counties. As Wisconsin returns the tax to the county, city or town in which it was collected, it frequently happened that income received within a locality is earned over a wider area and it results in the concentration of an excessive amount of revenue in one locality at the expense of others. When any county receives more revenue than is needed, waste often results. This is particularly true when as in Wisconsin the re-

[1] Holcomb, "State Income Taxes—Safeguarding the Yield—Methods employed in Delaware," *National Tax Association Bulletin*, vol. vi, no. 4, January 1921, p. 126.

[2] A. Comstock, *State Taxation of Personal Income*, New York, 1921, p. 201.

turn is from an income tax which includes both individual and corporate incomes. So the law further specifies that "when such balance exceeds two per cent of the equalized value of such town, city or village, the excess shall be paid to the county to be distributed to the towns, cities and counties according to the school population." [1]

The discussion of the proportions and the difficulties arising from them has taken into consideration to a limited extent the basis for return. In the first Massachusetts law the basis for distribution makes it quite obvious that the reason for returning a share to the local districts was to replace the revenue lost when personal property could no longer be taxed by the local district. The revenue is to be divided so that the amount paid to each city or town was to be an "amount equal to the difference between the amount of the tax levied upon personal property in such city or town in the year 1915 and the amount, computed by the tax commissioner, that would be produced by a tax assessed in such city or town for the year 1917, at the same rate of taxation as prevailed therein in the year 1915." [2] Later Massachusetts changed its basis of return. The law of 1919 provided that the amount returned on the original basis should be gradually decreased, until it reached ten per cent in 1927. In 1928 and thereafter the distribution should be made on the basis of assessed valuation of property in each city and town.[3] The method used in New York is to return the revenue on the basis of assessed value of real estate. In both cases the state is reapportioning the revenue to different localities, partially for the purpose of raising and equalizing the assessments in the different counties. New Hampshire, Tennessee and Wisconsin all return the revenue on the basis of residence of

[1] *Wisconsin Statutes*, 1925, ch. 52, sec. 71.19.

[2] *Massachusetts Statutes*, 1916, ch. 269, sec. 23.

[3] *Massachusetts Statutes*, 1919, ch. 314, p. 296.

the owner of the taxable income, which would mean returning the tax to the place where it was collected. The difficulty arising from this last method has already been referred to in the discussion of Wisconsin's experience.

In New York the attempt to equalize assessments by returning the revenue according to the assessed valuation has not been entirely successful. Mr. Gulick, in his appraisal of the New York tax system says:

> But with all this, the state of New York is very far indeed from achieving substantial fairness in local assessments. The discrimination as between individuals unquestionably represents many millions of dollars. Assessments in some jurisdictions are evidently still political, and equalization in many counties is still a matter of political power, tempered by the fear of certiorari proceedings.[1]

The Wisconsin basis for reapportionment was given in the discussion of proportions. In three of the five laws discussed the basis is assessed valuation supplemented in some cases by educational needs as the basis for the surplus.

On the whole, the revenue from the income tax has been returned with few requirements as to how it shall be spent. The reason for this is that the sharing has been to replace what was taken from the local districts. It was only with the development of a surplus that Wisconsin prescribed the use of money for the schools. The early New York law did require that the money going to New York City should be used " to reduce taxes ",[2] but this was a regulation to prevent the local districts from keeping the same rate of taxes as when the state tax had been added to the local tax on personal property. In 1921 New York, probably because of

[1] Gulick, "Tax System of New York," *National Tax Association Proceedings*, vol. xxii, 1929, p. 81.

[2] *New York Statutes*, 1919, ch. 627, sec. 382.

the large amount which was returned, required that one-third of the town funds should be paid to the school districts, but in 1922 changed this to an optional use of the towns funds to be decided upon by the town board.[1]

There seems to be no doubt that the income tax should be a state-administered tax, but the question as to whether or not it should be shared with the locality is not so clear. The committee of the National Tax Association on Model Taxation states that it is immaterial to its plan whether the state keeps all the revenue or shares it.

> It is probable, furthermore, that the same solution may not be advisable in every state. If the state should keep the entire revenue, then every section of the state would benefit to the extent that such revenue might reduce the direct state tax. On the other hand, if the revenue from the income tax is distributed wholly to local units, as is now the case in Massachusetts, the lightening of local burdens tends to reduce the pressure of the direct state tax.[2]

However, Professor Comstock does not agree entirely with the committee, for she replies to the above contention:

> This is undeniably true, but in this matter, as in many other instances, the actual reliefs or burdens conferred through the operation of taxes are extremely likely to be assumed by the least intelligent of the taxpayers to remain where they first fall. Hence a better understanding on the part of the average taxpayer of the actual effect of the income tax is obtained if at least a part of the proceeds is distributed to the local unit where the taxpayer resides. Furthermore, the distribution should be made with such a purpose and in such a way that the taxpayer is made conscious of the lightening of his burden.[3]

[1] *New York Statutes*, 1921, ch. 477, p. 1431; 1923, ch. 897, p. 1734.

[2] "Preliminary Report of the Committee on a Model System of Taxation," *National Tax Association*, vol. xvi, New York, 1923, p. 443.

[3] Comstock, *op. cit.*, p. 205.

The point made by Professor Comstock and the additional fact that many taxes do take away from the basis of taxation for the local government make it desirable that the returns from this tax should be shared with the local district.

The National Tax Association committee suggests in case of division that the state government might keep an amount equal to the proportion that state expenditures are to total state and local expenditures. In none of the laws has this suggestion been followed.

In so far as we may draw conclusions from five instances only, the local sharing of the income tax seems to mean reapportionment of revenue according to whatever principle the state wishes to stress. There seems to be only a slight tendency to dictate terms for the use of the money so that division of the income tax carries with it a slight control over the local units.

Except in a few cases where the locality is compensated for lost revenue there is no reason why this particular tax should be shared with the local districts except that it is one of the largest sources of tax revenue which the state is tapping and the localities do need money. However, returning a fixed percentage from a tax which varies as much in yield as the income tax does is questionable procedure.

CHAPTER VII

State-Administered Locally-Shared Forest and Severance Taxes

FOREST TAXES

The taxation of forest land is a special problem of the general property tax. Those interested in forest preservation and fair taxation of property have long recognized the forest tax as a special problem because it is a "fifty-year crop". To quote Professor Fairchild, from the report of the Committee to study Forest Taxation, "The property tax is fundamentally defective when applied to the total value of land and trees of a growing forest, resulting, if strictly administered, in grossly excessive taxation of forests as compared with other forms of property yielding annual income." [1] "The old general property tax was defective because (a) by taxing the total value of land and trees it imposed an excessive burden upon the growing forest, and (b) it placed on the owner the inconvenient obligation of paying annual taxes for years before any income was realized." [2]

He suggests a classification of forest lands so that they are assessed at a lower rate for the general property tax while growing plus a yield tax or an income tax at the time of cutting. The yield tax will of necessity be irregular, and therefore he suggests that the state pay the town's share of taxes from year to year, and then be reimbursed

[1] Fairchild, "Report of the Committee on Forest Taxation," *National Tax Association Proceedings*, vol. xv, 1922, pp. 128-9.

[2] *Ibid.*, p. 135.

when the timber is cut, or that the forest tax be a state tax and have the state surrender some other source of income to the locality.

This would mean, first of all, classification of property, and, since many states have the uniformity rule, it has necessarily been a slow change to get anything approximating this system. The number of states having special forest legislation in 1929 was twenty-six. Of these six have taxes which are locally shared. The total amount of the revenue shared in 1928 by these six taxes was $65,183.

Forest tax legislation providing for the sharing of taxes has been very recent. The first law which shared the revenue with the local districts was that of Indiana in 1921. This tax was one hundred per cent of the unearned increment on the value of the land between the time of classification and the time of withdrawal. All of the taxes follow Professor Fairchild's suggestion, and provide for low assessments on forest land for the ordinary property tax, thus depriving the local units of some tax revenue while the forest is growing. The local units receive compensation for this loss by sharing the yield tax when the timber is harvested. Michigan has, in addition to the yield tax, two other taxes. —a specific fixed land tax and a withdrawal fee, both of which are shared.

The proportions returned vary. Idaho returned one hundred per cent of the tax to the localities to replace the loss in the property tax; Alabama, Indiana, Louisiana, and Michigan return between ninety-nine and fifty per cent. Not only do these states return a smaller proportion of the tax than Idaho, but they also tax less; for example, Alabama has a ten per cent stumpage tax and returns fifty per cent to the counties, while Idaho has a twelve and one-half per cent stumpage tax and returns one hundred per cent to the county. There is no standard of what is a fair return, but each state does what it considers adequate. In Wisconsin all the revenue over ten cents per acre per year for the time the forest was classified is returned to the counties in proportion to the taxes they would have had if the land had not been classified. This is taken to be what it would have paid if the forest had been assessed as other property and paid the regular rate. Michigan's specific tax (a form of property tax) goes one hundred per cent to the county, which in turn gives seventy-five per cent to the town and the town gives seventy-five per cent of its share to the school districts. The withdrawal fee is divided equally between the county and the state.

There have been no changes in the proportions returned from any of these taxes, nor have there been any requirements for the spending of the revenue. This is probably because the taxes are really property taxes paid at the time the timber is cut rather than throughout the growing period, and until there are requirements on spending of the property tax, this form of sharing will undoubtedly remain unallocated by the state.

SEVERANCE TAXES

In the taxation of mines, oil and gas products we have another special problem of the general property tax, but it differs from the forest problem in that the natural resources are not capable of being renewed, whereas the forest crop grows again. The right to sever natural resources is considered a special privilege, and therefore the company or person severing these resources is liable to a special benefit tax as well as the regular property tax. State assessment of this property, however, is necessary, since the assessment requires, more than any other, trained experts to do the work. Where the local districts near the mines or oil fields are largely dependent upon the industries for revenue the tax should be locally shared.

TABLE IX

PRESENT STATUS OF STATE-ADMINISTERED LOCALLY-SHARED FOREST TAX LAWS, 1929

State	Law first dividing revenue	Jurisdiction administering	Designated use	Percentage to local district	Basis of distribution
Alabama	1923	State Commissioner of Forestry	..	50 to counties	Where forest is located
Idaho	1929	County supervised by State	..	100 to counties	Where collected
Indiana	1921	Conservation Commission	..	50 to counties 25 to towns	Where collected
Michigan	1925	Commissioner of Conservation	..	*Stumpage* 50 to counties *Specific*[a] 100 to counties *Withdrawal* 50 to counties	 Where property is located Where property is located Where property is located
Wisconsin	1927	State Treasurer	..	Amount yearly real estate tax above 10 cents per acre per year during growing period, plus 5 per cent interest to towns and counties	In proportion to what respective units of government would have received if land had paid regular property tax, and in same proportion

[a] Divided again.

There were fifteen severance taxes in the different states in 1929, of which five are shared with the local districts. In Oklahoma and Michigan it is in lieu of any other state or local property taxes, and therefore returned to local districts to replace the property tax. In Arkansas, Louisiana and Montana the tax is a franchise tax in addition to the property tax, but is probably returned simply because the locality demands a share in this source of revenue and can get it through its political power.

Taxation of the severance of natural resources in a special way is a comparatively new movement. The first law in which a severance tax was shared was the Oklahoma law of 1915, followed in 1923 by Arkansas, Louisiana and Montana, and in 1929 by Michigan.

Except for the new Michigan law which returns sixty per cent of the tax to counties, cities and towns the proportion returned is at present never more than thirty-three and one-third per cent. The original Oklahoma law returned fifty per cent to the localities, but changed it the next year to thirty-three and one-third per cent. The Louisiana law, which was originally a return of thirty-three and one-third per cent of the tax, has returned only twenty per cent since 1928. Montana gives back twenty-five per cent of the tax.

The revenue is returned where collected, except in the case of Montana, where it is returned to the county and district high schools on the basis of the aggregate number of days of school attendance during the preceding school year. Oklahoma originally reapportioned it according to the number of school children in each county, but since 1916 it has returned it to the county from which it came, as do Arkansas, Louisiana and Michigan.

In every case except Michigan, the purpose for which the revenue is to be used is specified as either for schools or roads. Arkansas and Oklahoma give fifty per cent of the revenue for roads in the county where collected. The other fifty per cent of these revenues and all the revenue of the other severance taxes which are shared by the states, except the Michigan tax, are designated for schools. Michigan makes no requirements as to the spending of the revenue.

None of the forest taxes and none of the severance taxes

except the Montana severance tax reapportion the revenue which is shared. The severance tax is used, however, to influence to a certain extent school expenditures, whereas the forest taxes are returned to general revenue, and leave the local districts free. The severance tax has only a slight tendency to influence local expenditures, for the return is a very small portion of the total educational expenditure, and it is returned for general educational needs.

TABLE X

PRESENT STATUS OF STATE-ADMINISTERED LOCALLY-SHARED SEVERANCE TAX LAWS, 1929

State	Law first dividing revenue	Jurisdiction administering	Designated use	Percentage to local district	Basis of distribution
Arkansas	1923	State Tax Commissioner	½ schools ½ highway fund	33⅓ to counties	Where collected
Louisiana	1923	Parish, supervised by State	Parish schools	20 to parishes[a]	Where collected
Michigan	1929	State Tax Commission	. .	20 to counties, 40 to cities or towns	Where collected
Montana	1923	State Treasurer	County and district high schools	25 to counties	In proportion to aggregate number days attendance during preceding school year
Oklahoma	1915	State Auditor	½ county schools; ½ road and bridge fund	33⅓ to counties[a]	Where collected

[a] Divided again.

TABLE XI

PRESENT STATUS OF STATE-ADMINISTERED LOCALLY-SHARED MISCELLANEOUS TAX LAWS, 1929

State	Law first dividing revenue	Jurisdiction administering	Designated use	Percentage to local district	Basis of distribution
Arizona	State road fund 1912 special property tax state road fund	State Treasurer	Construction and repair of roads	75 to counties	Where collected
Arkansas	Mining records 1895	County Treasurer supervised by State	County record fund	50 to counties	Where collected
Connecticut	Unincorporated business 1925	Tax Commissioner	..	50 to counties	Proportion population of county bears to whole state according to United States Census
	Choses in action 1915	Tax Commission	..	80 to towns or cities	Where decedent lived
Iowa	Cigarette tax 1927	State Treasurer	..	100 to cities and towns	Where collected
Kansas	Secured debts 1927	State Treasurer	..	16⅔ to counties; 33⅓ to city or town; 33⅓ to school district	According to assessed valuation
Maine	Dog license 1893	County supervised by State	..	100 to towns after damage done by dogs is paid	Where collected
Massachusetts	Boxing fees 1920	Boxing Commission	..	100 to cities and towns	Where collected
New York	Billiard and pool room license 1922	State Tax Commission	..	50 to cities, towns and villages	Where collected
	Real estate brokers license 1922	Department of State	..	50 to counties[a]	Where collected

[a] Divided again.

TABLE XI—*Concluded*

State	Law first dividing revenue	Jurisdiction administering	Designated use	Percentage to local district	Basis of distribution
North Dakota	Billiard and pool room license 1921	State Licensing Department	..	70 to villages, cities and towns	Where collected
South Dakota	Money and credit 1919	County supervised by State	..	50 to counties, 25 to school district	Where assessed
Vermont	Peddlers' license 1857	County supervised by State	..	100 to counties	According to population

CHAPTER VIII

State-Administered Locally-Shared Taxes Abroad

Other countries have attempted to solve the problem of the adjustment of state and local functions to state and local revenue in varying ways. The difference in the political systems abroad results in a somewhat different problem from that in this country. However, a brief summary of the French, English and German systems will show how these countries are trying to meet the problems under discussion.

The situation in Germany approximates that of the United States for the German Reich is a federal government. Before and during the war, under the German tax system, the largest part of the taxes was administered by the states and communes which contributed to the national government. After the Weimar constitution the scope of the taxing power of the Reich was enlarged, and under the law of March 30, 1920, the financial relations of the Reich with the states and communes were radically changed. Whereas before the states and communes had levied most of their own taxes, the Reich now took over the administration of most of the taxes and gave a share to the states and communes.[1] In 1913-14 the Reich collected 39.1 per cent of the total tax revenues of Germany while the states, communes and Hanseatic Cities collected 60.9 per cent of the taxes.[2] The effect of the new law was to reverse the position of the Reich and the state and local governments as agencies of tax collection. Collections by the Reich were 68 per cent of the total tax

[1] *Report of the Agent General for Reparation Payments*, London, July 1, 1929, p. 75.

[2] *Ibid.*, p. 82.

collections in 1925-6 and nearly 70 per cent in 1927-8 and the first half of 1928-9.[1]

In spite of the fact that the Reich collects a much larger proportion of the revenues, it expends only a slightly larger proportion than in prewar times. In 1913-4 the Reich expended 40.2 per cent of the total German revenues and since 1925 has been spending between 42.3 per cent and 44.3 per cent of the total.[2] This increase in the collection of tax revenue with no corresponding increase in expenditures by the Reich means, of course, a compensating change in the collection and expenditures of the states and communes. Their collections are at present about 30 per cent of the tax revenues and their expenditures about 56 per cent of the total.[3]

A table of sources of revenue in the Agent General's report discloses the fact that not only has the Reich control changed the administration of taxation, but it has also changed the sources of the taxes for the states and communes. In 1913-14 the states and communes each received about one-half of their taxes from the income and corporation taxes; the states now receive 43 per cent from these sources and the communes 23 per cent. The states and communes receive the difference from the nationally administered real estate transaction and occupation taxes and the new taxes on rent and turnover.[4] This rather complete control by the national government is summed up in the following recent discussion of government and administration in Germany.

> At present the Reich administers not only all the taxes and customs which appertain to the national treasury; but several others

[1] *Ibid.*, p. 82.

[2] *Ibid.*, p. 82.

[3] *Ibid.*, p. 82.

[4] *Ibid.*, p. 82.

which, though nominally national taxes, are turned over to the states and municipalities *in toto* except for a small deduction to cover the cost of collection. Moreover, it exercises a very great degree of control over the state and municipalities in respect to tax regulation and tax administration. It is even empowered by law to administer the taxation systems of the state and municipalities if they so desire.[1]

The taxes transferred to the states and communes are divided into two groups, the proportional transfers and special payments. These transfers were originated by the law of March 30, 1920, in compliance with the Weimar Constitution, which required that if the Reich took over taxes and revenues of the states it was to pay due regard to the ability of the states to maintain themselves. The proportional transfers are by far the largest part of the transfers to states and communes and are the result of a series of provisional settlements between the Reich and the states and communes. The arrangement in 1929 was that the Reich was to give the states and communes 75 per cent of the yield of the income and corporation taxes, 30 per cent of the yield of the turnover tax and 96 per cent of the yield of the taxes on real estate transactions, automobiles and race-betting. The Reich has also made special arrangements with certain states to give special payments (1) to states which on the basis of proportional transfers receive unfavorable treatment (amount paid in 1929 about 30 millions of reichsmarks), (2) to states whose base of taxation was decreased by the amalgamation of companies (in 1929 there was no return on this basis) and (3) to Bavaria, Würtemburg and Baden which receive a share of the beer tax (not more than fifty-nine millions of reichsmarks in 1929).[2]

[1] Blachly and Oatman, *The Government and Administration of Germany*, Maryland, 1928, p. 184.

[2] *Report of the Agent General on Reparation Payments, op. cit.*, 1929, p. 52.

The description of these taxes shows the proportional tax transfers to be very similar to the state-administered locally-shared taxes of the United States in that they are collected by a higher authority and turned back to a smaller district and in that they are proportional returns and, therefore, vary in amount with the yield of the tax. The special payments are somewhat similar to the state-administered locally-shared taxes in that they are a return for revenues surrendered by the local districts but they are different in being an adjusted amount rather than a proportional return.

The percentage which the proportional transfers and special payments were of the total state revenue averages 62 per cent in 1928-29 for all states and varies from 77 per cent in Saxony to 41 per cent in Hamburg. The revenue which was in turn transferred to the communes by the states and Hanseatic Cities averaged 40 per cent of the total revenue of the states and the Hanseatic Cities and varies from 49 per cent transferred by Prussia to 2 per cent transferred by Hamburg.[1]

The Reich has made little attempt to redistribute or to dictate the use of the revenues among the states. For example, in the case of the income tax, it is to be a share equal to what the state got from this source before the change. In case the state is not satisfied with its share, it protests to the Minister of Finance.[2] The states, however, have considerable control over the communes, for they are to decide what the needs of the communes are and return revenues accordingly. The states are to give consideration to the poorer communes in redistributing the income, corporation and turnover taxes.[3]

There is, however, no attempt on the part of the national

[1] *Ibid.*, p. 85.

[2] Blachly and Oatman, *op. cit.*, p. 186.

[3] *Ibid.*, p. 187.

government in deciding how much revenue to give the states and communes to relate the resources of the states and communes to their obligations. This leads to great waste of revenue when the states and communes receive more revenue than they need and serious curtailment of functions when they receive less than their accustomed income. This is particularly serious when the national government is in such severe financial straits as it is at present. The report of the Agent General of Reparations in 1926 states most clearly the difficulty of the financial relations between the Reich and the states and communes.

The present system, however, is far from satisfactory, and it is difficult to see how it can last. It takes from the Reich, without relation to the actual needs of the states and communes, a heavy percentage of the revenue it collects, and worst of all, it takes the bulk of the income and corporation taxes, the very ones that are most responsive to the development of business and industry and that should be most available to meet the obligations of the Reich itself. In this sense, it still "constitutes a constant drain upon federal resources," and a "hole in the budget that must be plugged." Even from the point of view of the states and communes the arrangements now in force have their disadvantages. In flush times, as, for example, in the year 1924-25, the states and communes, whose needs are fairly constant, receive transfers of revenue far in excess of their real requirements. This, in itself, promptly tempts them into new expenditures, and sometimes to extravagance. Then, when times become more difficult and transfers from the Reich tend to shrink the states and communes find themselves under pressure to meet their increased expenditures and return to the Reich for further aid. Thus the practice grows, neither the Reich nor the states and communes are satisfied and expenditures continue to mount. For the taxpayer the result must be entirely disagreeable, and it would seem that from his point of view at least it would be better far to have a system which more clearly defined the responsibility for levying taxes and placed it squarely on the shoulders of the governing body responsible in the first instance for the expenditure.[1]

Commenting on this difficulty again in his 1929 report, the Agent General states that in 1928-29 the transfers to the states and communes absorbed 74 per cent of the total increase in tax revenue of the Reich, an increase which the Reich itself sorely needed.[2]

Not only does the Reich return large sums of money, but it has also assumed some of the functions formerly performed by the local districts. "The Reich, on the other hand, while paying over increasing amounts from its tax revenues to the states and communes, has not only relieved them entirely of their former liabilities in respect of ordinary unemployment relief, . . . but has itself undertaken the burden of many national adjustments arising out of the war. . . ."[3]

That Germany is aware of the evils of the situation and is attempting to remedy them is evident in the 1929 provisional fiscal settlement between the Reich and the smaller districts. The law of March 31, 1929, provides for the retention by the Reich of 120 million marks from the income, corporation and turnover taxes if the total of the three is more than 4,530 million marks. Commenting on this, the Agent General says:

The net effect of this provision of the budget law is to reduce by 71 millions at the maximum the amount which will be transferred to the states and communes. While the amount of the

[1] *Report of the Agent General for Reparation Payments*, Berlin, November, 1926, p. 36.

[2] *Report of the Agent General for Reparation Payments, op. cit.*, 1929, p. 53.

[3] *Ibid.*, p. 54.

reduction is small, it has some importance as representing, for the first time in nearly four years, a practical step in the direction of checking the steady increase in transfers to the states and the communes; and it shows an effort to give some consideration to the requirements of the budget of the Reich.[1]

The German tax system is a much more highly centralized system than that of the United States. The Reich turns over to the states a large proportion of their revenues. There is nothing comparable in the United States. Except for the state offset in the federal estate tax mentioned in the chapter on the inheritance taxes, our federal government administers no taxes for the benefit of the states. The German states turn over to the communes 40.0 per cent of the revenue received from the Reich. This is a much larger percentage than the 17.4 per cent which the states in this country give to the local districts. This extreme case shows the difficulties which are apt to appear if some basic principles are not applied to the solution of the problem. That political expediency requires some return to be made to local districts must be remembered, but with this return must go regulation. It does not seem necessary to have the return a fixed proportion of a tax. This brings the difficulties which arise from fluctuating amounts of revenue.

In the case of Germany the present extreme centralization is to be explained as a compromise of post-war financing. It may be temporary but according to some students of the situation the restriction on state and local self-determination in matters of taxation is deeply rooted.[2]

In France we find a highly centralized form of government, but the taxes which are somewhat similar to those studied in this problem are such a small fraction of the total tax system that they have not become a real problem.

[1] *Ibid.*, p. 54.

[2] Blachly and Oatman, *op. cit.*, p. 217.

For administrative purposes France is divided into ninety departments and many thousands of communes. The department has little independence, the prefect who had charge of the department being nominated by the central government. The prefect, then, is really a representative of the executive, and he appoints the officials who decide the commune's quota of direct taxation.[1] There seems to be none of the local autonomy of the United States in the French system. It is to be expected in consequence that the finances of all divisions of government will be closely allied.

As to the sources of local taxes, Professor Haig gives the following information:

> In the first place an important part of the local revenues flows from the so-called *centimes additionnels*, which are taxes levied upon a basis originally established for national purposes. A second important part of the local revenue finds its source in grants and subventions from the national treasury to départements and communes. Then, in contrast with these payments flowing from larger divisions to the smaller, the départements receive large payments from the communes and the national government receives small payments from both.[2]

The taxes which are shared by the departments and the communes are: first, the *fonds communes,* which are collected by the state. In 1926 the departments received 170 million francs from this source and the communes received an additional 733 million francs.[3] The departments and communes receive each year the proceeds of this tax fund.

The manner in which they share in this fund of state-collected taxes is radically different. The arrangement, with the approx-

[1] *Statesman's Year Book*, London, 1930, p. 846.

[2] R. M. Haig, *The Public Finances of Post-War France*, New York, 1929, pp. 364-5.

[3] *Ibid.*, pp. 387 and 388.

imate share of the communes in the collections, is as follows: (1) the turnover tax proper (3.33 per cent) and the coal-extraction tax (4 per cent); (2) the charge for *cartes d'identité* for foreigners (10 per cent of the 100 franc tax and 12½ per cent of the 20 franc tax); and (3) the tax on beverages—wines, cider, perry, hydromel (26⅔ per cent), diluted wine (*piquette*) (66⅔ per cent), beer (25 per cent), alcohol (specific tax) 19 per cent.[1]

The second group of taxes is a group of different types of taxes which are part of the *taxes assimilees, i.e.*, taxes assimilated with the direct taxes. Among these are the proportional tax on mine profits (22 per cent) and the tax on carriages and horses.[2] In 1926 the amount the communes received from these taxes was 22 million francs. This makes a total of 925 million francs received by the departments and communes from the state, which is 12.4 per cent of the total taxes of the departments and communes. This 925 million francs was 2 per cent of total state, department and commune taxes in 1926.[3] The comparatively small amount of these taxes makes them relatively unimportant in the French tax system.

In France, then, the question discussed in this paper is not of primary importance, since the sub-divisions of finance are essentially part of the national system, and since the part contributed by these taxes is relatively a small part of the local revenue system. Although the shares returned vary with the yield of the tax inasmuch as they are percentage returns, fluctuations in yield do not cause a serious problem, owing to their relative unimportance.

The relation of the central government in England to the local units is neither as bureaucratic as that of France and

[1] *Ibid.*, p. 388.

[2] *Ibid.*, p. 388, footnote.

[3] *Ibid.*, pp. 375, 379, 397.

Germany nor as casual as that of the United States. Early English government tended to be nearly as chaotic as that in the United States, but during the nineteenth century there was a gradual realization that some check upon local authorities was necessary to keep them from spending taxes unwisely and mortgaging the future too heavily. Furthermore, as in any developing country, the increase in population made problems of health, roads and other functions more than local problems. This historical development of England is described by Mr. Webb in his book on "Grants in Aid."

> The National Government, in the course of the three-quarters of a century from 1832, successively "bought" the rights of inspection, audit, supervision, initiative, criticism, and control, in respect of one local service after another, and of one kind of local governing body after another, by the grant of annual subventions from the National Exchequer in aid of the local finances, and therefore, in relief of the local rate-payer.[1]

The subventions mentioned by Mr. Webb take many different forms and are granted on different bases, but there is nothing comparable in England to the state-administered locally-shared taxes in the United States. The subvention, or "grant-in-aid", is an essential part of the central control of local government in England, and is of growing fiscal importance. In 1928-9 13.4 per cent of the total national tax revenues were disbursed in this way. In 1929-30 this percentage had increased to 16.6.[2]

Certain suggestions from these foreign surveys seem worthy of consideration in connection with our own problem. England is frankly supervising and controlling the

[1] S. Webb, *Grants in Aid: A Criticism and a Proposal*, London, 1920, p. 6.

[2] Compiled from data in *Statesman's Year Book*, 1930, pp. 34-35.

local expenditure of the money which she returns. It is like the subvention in the United States, a method which is used in the United States to only a limited extent. While the subvention is less apt to lead to extravagance or insufficient help than the state-administered locally-shared tax, it can hardly replace entirely the state-administered locally-shared taxes, as long as this country still favors a large amount of local autonomy. It does, however, seem feasible to urge that a subvention replace part of the taxes now shared so that the sums returned to local governments will be more in accordance with needs. The German situation points to the danger of letting the present tendency to increase state-administered locally-shared taxes go too far before some fundamental principles are established to serve as a guide in determining the amount and kind of revenues returned.

CHAPTER IX

Summary and Conclusions

That state-administered locally-shared taxes are a vital and growing part of the present tax system cannot be denied.[1] The revenues received from all such taxes increased from $186,640,000 in 1925 to $261,220,000 in 1928. In 1925 they amounted to 4.1 per cent of the total local tax revenue; in 1928 they increased to 5.6 per cent. In 1928 the revenue returned by this method was 17.4 per cent of the total state tax revenues. The increasing number of laws and the increasing importance of these revenues in the local budgets demonstrate that this movement is developing rapidly. The increase in the amount obtained by these taxes is owing both to the fact that first, the states are continually increasing the rates of these taxes, making an increase in the total receipts, and therefore in the share the localities receive; and secondly, there is an increasing number of taxes which have become state-administered locally-shared taxes. (See Table I, Chapter II).

The following tables show the extent to which each state uses this particular form of taxation:

[1] "The state-administered tax which is returned to the municipality is of much more importance than the state-controlled locally-administered tax. Not only are the amounts involved much larger, but the state-administered taxes are increasing at a rapid rate. They represent the newer and larger tax sources. Furthermore, they indicate a more far-reaching control." Newcomer, "Tendencies in State and Local Finance and their Relation to State and Local Functions," *Political Science Quarterly*, vol. xliii, no. 1, March, 1928, pp. 17-8.

TABLE XII [a]

NUMBER OF STATE-ADMINISTERED LOCALLY-SHARED TAXES IN ALL STATES, NUMBER REAPPORTIONED, AND NUMBER IN WHICH THE USE IS DESIGNATED, 1929

State	Total number of state-administered locally-shared taxes	Number of taxes reapportioned	Number of taxes having designated use
Alabama	4	2	2
Arizona	2	—	2
Arkansas	3	—	3
California	3	2	3
Colorado	4	2	4
Connecticut	4	4	—
Delaware	—	—	—
Florida	6	5	3
Georgia	1	1	1
Idaho	3	—	1
Illinois	1	1	1
Indiana	2	1	1
Iowa	4	3	2
Kansas	5	3	2
Kentucky	1	1	—
Louisiana	4	1	3
Maine	3	2	—
Maryland	5	4	3
Massachusetts	5	4	—
Michigan	5	1	2
Minnesota	4	1	1
Mississippi	2	1	2
Missouri	1	1	1
Montana	3	2	3
Nebraska	2	1	2
Nevada	1	1	1
New Hampshire	5	2	—
New Jersey	4	3	1
New Mexico	2	1	2
New York	8	3	2
North Carolina	2	1	1
North Dakota	5	1	3
Ohio	4	2	4
Oklahoma	4	1	4
Oregon	2	1	2
Pennsylvania	2	—	1

[a] Compiled from data in Tables IV through XI.

State	Total number of state-administered locally-shared taxes	Number of taxes reapportioned	Number of taxes having designated use
Rhode Island ..	—	—	—
South Carolina .	3	2	2
South Dakota ..	4	—	2
Tennessee	2	1	1
Texas	2	—	2
Utah	—	—	—
Vermont	1	1	—
Virginia	2	2	2
Washington ...	3	2	2
West Virginia .	—	—	—
Wisconsin	7	2	1
Wyoming	2	2	1
Total	142	71	76

TABLE XIII[a]

AMOUNT OF STATE TAX REVENUE FROM STATE-ADMINISTERED LOCALLY-SHARED TAXES RETURNED IN EACH STATE, 1928

(In thousands of dollars)

State	Total state taxes	Local revenue from state-administered locally-shared taxes: Total		Reapportioned		Use designated	
		Amount	Per cent of state taxes	Amount	Per cent of locally-shared taxes	Amount	Per cent of locally-shared taxes
Alabama	20,766	4,268	20.6	4,256	99.7	3,884	91.0
Arizona	7,962	76	1.0	—	—	76	100.0
Arkansas	15,581	397	2.6	—	—	397	100.0
California	81,465	13,867	17.0	9,835	70.9	13,867	100.0
Colorado	13,391	1,996	14.9	1,241	62.2	1,996	100.0
Connecticut	27,983	3,300	11.8	3,300	100.0	—	—
Delaware	7,345	—	—	—	—	—	—
Florida	20,894	3,605	17.3	835	23.2	3,547	98.4
Georgia	20,719	2,035	9.8	2,035	100.0	2,035	100.0
Idaho	4,842	2,635	54.4	—	—	2,635	100.0
Illinois	70,525	9,200	13.0	9,200	100.0	9,200	100.0
Indiana	33,067	3,683	11.1	3,647	99.0	3,644	98.9
Iowa	29,570	13,554	45.9	13,326	98.3	10,084	74.4

[a] Data from reports of state auditors, treasurers, tax commissioners and comptrollers.

State	Total state taxes	Local revenue from state-administered locally-shared taxes: Total		Reapportioned		Use designated	
		Amount	Per cent of state taxes	Amount	Per cent of locally-shared taxes	Amount	Per cent of locally-shared taxes
Kansas	19,768	3,035	15.4	2,826	93.1	2,836	93.4
Kentucky	25,043	481	1.9	481	100.0	—	—
Louisiana	22,021	1,077 [b]	4.9	628 [b]	58.3	1,077 [b]	100.0
Maine	15,721	196	1.2	183	93.4	—	—
Maryland	20,003	2,390	11.9	2,347	98.2	2,163	90.5
Massachusetts .	45,105	37,590	83.3	37,560	99.9	—	—
Michigan	78,664	9,825	12.5	2,813	28.6	7,813	79.5
Minnesota	42,947	410	1.0	56	13.6	233	56.8
Mississippi	11,185	5,178	46.3	2,748	53.1	5,178	100.0
Missouri	34,030	1,160	3.4	1,160	100.0	1,160	100.0
Montana	6,157	2,466	40.1	1,284	52.1	2,466	100.0
Nebraska	17,133	2,805	16.4	—	—	2,805	100.0
Nevada	2,049	279	13.6	279	100.0	279	100.0
New Hampshire	7,324	1,581	21.6	409	25.9	—	—
New Jersey	74,861	14,365	19.2	13,007	90.5	2,202	15.3
New Mexico ...	8,333	388	4.7	49	12.6	388	100.0
New York	207,773	62,667	30.2	46,167	73.7	29,439	47.0
North Carolina .	32,138	14	.04	—	—	—	—
North Dakota ..	7,863	830	10.6	—	—	748	90.1
Ohio	57,281	17,430	30.4	9,187	52.7	16,169	92.8
Oklahoma	22,010	9,807	44.5	2,518	25.7	9,807	100.0
Oregon	18,599	1,682	9.0	40	2.4	1,682	100.0
Pennsylvania ..	120,547	4,382	3.6	—	—	3,605	82.3
Rhode Island ...	9,641	—	—	—	—	—	—
South Carolina .	16,174	1,919	11.9	1,734	90.4	1,734	90.4
South Dakota ..	10,458	332	3.2	—	—	96	28.9
Tennessee	19,655	1,836	9.3	1,836	100.0	1,836	100.0
Texas	70,041	7,279	10.4	—	—	7,279	100.0
Utah	8,480	—	—	—	—	—	—
Vermont	5,660	5	.1	5	100.0	—	—
Virginia	30,979	2,735	8.8	2,735	100.0	2,735	100.0
Washington ...	29,857	2,553	8.6	—	—	2,553	100.0
West Virginia .	18,803	—	—	—	—	—	—
Wisconsin	34,756	5,901	17.0	3,944	66.8	259	4.4
Wyoming	3,180	3	.1	3	100.0	—	—
Total	1,503,830	261,220	17.4	181,672	69.5	159,907	61.2

[b] 1927—Latest state figures available.

There are four states, Delaware, Rhode Island, Utah and West Virginia, which have none of these taxes, and forty-four states in which this form of taxation is a part of the state and local tax system. New York and Wisconsin, both of which are well advanced industrially, have more laws providing for state-administered locally-shared taxes than any other states. New York has eight such laws and Wisconsin has seven. New Hampshire and Florida each have six such laws. Two, three and four are the more usual number of laws, as there is usually a motor vehicle tax, a gasoline tax, and at least one corporation tax that the state shares. Of the corporation taxes, public utility and fire insurance company taxes are those most frequently shared.

There seems to be no special geographical region where the state-administered locally-shared tax predominates, nor is it peculiar to any type of industrial development. In New England, Rhode Island gives no revenue to the local districts by this method, whereas Massachusetts shares the largest proportion (83.3 per cent) of any state. Both of these are densely populated manufacturing states. The state sharing the second largest proportion of its revenue with the local district in this way is Idaho, a sparsely populated agricultural and mining state, while the neighboring mountain state of Utah, also a sparsely populated state with mining and agricultural interests predominating is one of the four states showing none. Idaho and Massachusetts are the only two states to give the local districts more than fifty per cent of their state revenues, and only four states: Iowa, Mississippi, Montana and Oklahoma, return between forty and fifty per cent of the state revenue through this type of tax law. Four states return between twenty and forty per cent of their revenues to the localities, and sixteen give between ten and twenty per cent. Eighteen states give the localities less than ten per cent of the total state revenue. In most states only a small part of the tax revenues are affected. It is to new taxes that the device is being widely applied, and these are rapidly increasing.

As has been said earlier, the outstanding reason why the taxes are shared is that the state is supplementing local revenue because it has taken from the localities some of the base of the property tax. This is especially true of the corporation tax and the personal income taxes. In levying these taxes part of the local tax base has been removed, and the state returns part of the revenue either from a sense of justice or as a political expedient. The motor transportation taxes are shared to aid the locality in building roads. The state recognizes good roads as more than a local matter, and is paying, therefore, part of the local road expenses. In some cases, also, this replaces lost local revenues. The inheritance tax is shared, probably, simply because the local districts need the money more than the state needs it, but as pointed out already,[1] it is doubtful whether this is a tax which should be shared. In the case of the severance and forest taxes it is a desire for efficiency which leads to placing the administration of these taxes in the hands of the state, and it is the benefit conferred by local government which causes them to be shared with the localities. The total amount returned from all of these taxes combined is a substantial addition to total local tax revenues.

Tables XII and XIII also give further information regarding the way in which this revenue is returned. Out of the 142 tax laws which return revenue, 71 return it to some place other than that from which it was collected. There are, then, 71 laws which return the revenue where it was collected. There is a decided tendency for the state to return the revenue according to some measure of local need. As mentioned in the introduction, the principal basis for re-

[1] *Cf. supra*, p. 61.

apportionment is some criterion of road needs. The situs of the property taxed is used to a large extent, and assessed valuation appears frequently. In few cases educational needs, population, or equal division were the bases used for reapportionment. All of these methods indicate increasing state control.

The total amount of revenue which is reapportioned is $181,672,000. This is 69.5 per cent of all the revenue returned from the state-administered locally-shared taxes. Ten states do not reapportion any of the revenue, but return it all where it is collected. These states are Arizona, Arkansas, Idaho, Nebraska, North Carolina, North Dakota, Pennsylvania, South Dakota, Texas and Washington. Most of the states reapportion one or two taxes. The exact number for each state is shown in Table XII. Of the states which reapportion the revenue there are ten which reapportion all that is returned. These states are Connecticut, Georgia, Illinois, Kentucky, Missouri, Nevada, Tennessee (does not reapportion 1929 income tax), Vermont, Virginia and Wyoming.

There are nine states, in addition to the ten reapportioning all the revenue, which reapportion more than ninety per cent of the total revenue returned; and only seven states of the thirty-four which reapportion any revenue that reapportion less than fifty per cent. These seven states are Florida, which redistributes 23.2 per cent, Michigan, which redistributes 28.6 per cent, Minnesota, 13.6 per cent, New Hampshire, 25.9 per cent, New Mexico, 12.6 per cent, Oklahoma, 25.7 per cent and Oregon, 2.4 per cent. In other words, if the state adopts the principle of reapportionment of revenue shared it usually does it for the major part of the revenue. The larger part of the revenue from state-administered locally-shared sources is state-controlled in that the state returns it according to some standard set by the state. Since the proportion of taxes reapportioned is not as large a part of the total taxes shared (71 out of 142, or 50 per cent) as the proportion of revenue is of the total revenue, ($181,-672,000 out of $261,220,000, or 69.5 per cent) it is evident that the states reapportion the more lucrative taxes.

The last point to bring out in this discussion of the effect of state-administered locally-shared taxes on the community is that 61.2 per cent of the total revenue returned is returned for a designated purpose. Referring to Table XII we find there are 76 state tax laws requiring specific use of the revenue returned. Ohio designates the use of revenue from four taxes, while the other states designate the use of fewer taxes. The only states which return the revenue of all taxes as free revenue are Connecticut, Kentucky, Maine, Massachusetts, New Hampshire and Vermont. These states are returning, in some cases, large sums of free revenue. For example, Massachusetts returned more than thirty-seven million dollars with no requirements as to how the local districts were to spend it. In 1928 $159,907,000 were returned from all states for designated uses. Although the large proportion of revenue returned for specific uses is indicative of a large amount of state control the localities still have the revenue from their own local property taxes. The designated revenue may be used for the purposes which the state directs, and thus leave whatever local revenue would have gone to those particular uses free for the local unit to spend as it wishes. However, as has been shown in the study of individual taxes, the amount so controlled, as well as the definiteness of the way in which the revenue is to be used, is giving the state increasing power in the direction and control of former local functions.

The lack of uniformity among the different taxes in the different states makes it difficult to generalize. Usually, however, the state-administered taxes replace some source of taxation taken from the locality. Further, the method lends itself to more and more state supervision, through reapportionment of the revenue according to the state's idea of need and through the establishment of minimum standards for the function for which the money is given. It is a movement to be watched, and studied, for the number of taxes so administered and returned is increasing and the revenue from them is an increasing proportion of the local tax receipts. The state sees the local need, and is giving its assistance, but with this assistance goes interference. This particular type of state interference will be questioned by believers in home rule, for it usually involves rigid legislative interference rather than flexible administrative control.

Another reason why those advocating home rule should be interested is that this may be a transitional stage of state control of the functions involved. There have been numerous instances of decreasing proportions given back to the locality, when the original return was undoubtedly made because of property taken away. An example of this is the reduction of the proportion returned from the Wisconsin income tax. The New Mexico car company tax is an instance of a tax once locally shared which now goes entirely to the state. If the state keeps an increasing share of the revenue and does not give the locality other revenues, the chances of the local district increasing its revenue are so negligible that it would seem to follow inevitably that the state will take over the functions formerly supported by this revenue.

There are certain advantages in having the state take over the functions and the revenues for the functions. Statewide assessment of most taxes except perhaps some local license taxes and the real estate tax in large cities is superior to local assessment in giving all equal treatment and in stopping evasion of taxation. It is also usually administered by more competent assessors for the state assessor is a higher salaried man and usually a full time, rather than a part time, official. Application of a uniform rate throughout the state means that there will be less shifting of business or residence within the state to escape taxation than otherwise.

Not only is the assessment usually done more efficiently by the state than by the local districts, but in many cases the governmental functions are more efficiently performed by the state. Certainly road building must have state-wide supervision to get a good state system of highways and the highways themselves may usually be better and more cheaply built if the state has the awarding of all roadbuilding contracts. State control of at least a minimum of education insures each citizen of that minimum. Another advantage of state control is the check on local extravagance and fraud. Not that state administration is free from fraud and extravagance, but the state government is more closely watched by the taxpayer. The state-administered locally-shared tax with increasing state control of the revenue has the advantages of more efficient tax administration and some of the efficiency of state control of local government.

That these efficiencies are real would seem to be indicated by the increase in state control in the face of home rule opposition. But it is this same home rule opposition which makes it necessary to proceed slowly and while proceeding, find definite justifiable standards by which to proceed.

Public opinion still favors local administration of certain functions. This same public opinion, as expressed in these laws providing for state-administered locally-shared taxes, indicates that the localities must be compensated for giving up the rights which they believe to be theirs. Mr. Kendrick, in writing of the situation in New York, gives some interesting examples of what he believes to be objective expression of the desire for local autonomy. He cites as one example the township school law of New York which was passed in 1917, placing the schools in each town under one governing board and providing that one tax rate should obtain for the entire town. Opposition to the measure began while it was being considered by the legislature and had become strong enough in 1918 to have the law repealed.

Not all of the opposition to this measure can be ascribed to a desire for local autonomy. Other reasons were included therein. Nevertheless, a reading of the documentary material assembled by the State Education Department establishes clearly that one of the main reasons for the overthrow of the township system was the desire for local autonomy.[1]

Another example of objective evidence of desire for local autonomy that Mr. Kendrick gives is the fact that the broad outlines of county and town governments in New York State remain today as in 1790 in spite of revolutionary social and economic changes which have altered radically every other social and economic institution in the state.[2]

The fact that the state-administered locally-shared taxes of each type vary so in the proportions returned is probably explained by the fact that what the local districts are able to get depends upon the political situation in each state. No practical suggestion can be made as to the proportion which should go back, as that will vary with the local needs and the state and local tax system of each state.

In considering the basis for the return of revenue, the taxes should be divided into three groups: the inheritance taxes, the motor transportation taxes, and all other taxes. The first group, inheritance taxes, should not be shared because there seems little justification for such a return and the great variation in yield tends to make it less suitable for

[1] M. S. Kendrick, *The Collection of Taxes by the State of New York and the Division of these Revenues with Units of Local Government*, New York, 1930, p. 22.

[2] *Ibid.*, p. 22.

local distribution. The reason for considering the motor transportation taxes separately is that these taxes are levied primarily on the benefit theory, and the expenditures of the local districts do benefit motor vehicle owners materially. In returning revenue to the cities these taxes should be returned on the double basis of mileage and motor vehicle registration in the cities, since there are the best measures of benefit. But in the case of the return to the counties and towns the method of subventions suggested above is advocated.[1] In the third group of taxes are the income taxes, the corporation taxes, and the forest and severance taxes. The local districts frequently have more claim to this type of revenue than to the revenue from the inheritance tax, but direct sharing of the yield of the individual taxes in this group seems distinctly inferior to the plan of making grants from the pooled revenues of all these taxes. If different methods of sharing are used for each tax it may well happen that the local district which receives a large amount for the taxes returned according to assessed valuation of property will receive a small amount from the taxes returned according to school needs. It seems a wiser policy to pool all of the returns of the different taxes and return the revenue to the local district according to one criterion. This would of necessity be a rather complicated formula. It should be based on the needs of the local district and should therefore, consider such things as population, taxable wealth, school children and health needs. Furthermore, the returns should be like subventions in that there should be a fixed amount each year. The state budget is better able to absorb differences in returns of different taxes than is the local district with its more limited resources. If the desire is to equalize the services received by the citizens of the state from the government (as it might well be assumed to be in a democracy),

[1] *Cf. supra*, p. 95.

the subvention might be such that, when added to the local taxes resulting from a fixed rate, each local district will have an equal share to spend per school child or per citizen or whatever base is used. This would insure the local district of at least a minimum. If the local district wishes to raise more money and have finer schools, parks or libraries, it is free to do so. One obvious objection to this plan is that opposition is usually encountered whenever revenues are diverted from one governmental unit to another. However, the chief difficulty in the redistribution would be in decreasing the funds paid to some districts in order to increase the funds paid to other districts. Only by adding considerable sums to the funds of revenue now distributed could the districts be assured of at least the amounts they now receive.

Before the subventions are made it would be necessary to consider carefully the governmental unit to which the money is to be returned. The unit should be small enough to satisfy the desire for local autonomy and it should be large enough to administer its functions efficiently.

There are cases in which collection should be considered as the basis of return. In so far as many taxes are more effectively administered by the state, taxes for local use, for example, local business taxes, e.g., a city tax on the amusement business, might be administered by the state to achieve greater efficiency and the revenue returned as a whole to the local district from which it was collected. In such cases the state would be merely administering the tax so that it would seem just to return such revenue to the place of collection.

If, however, it were necessary to choose between state usurpation of all local functions and the present system of state-administered locally-shared taxes there would be much to say for allowing the local district its present degree of freedom in spending revenue. But the possibility of substituting the state subvention for some of the shared taxes should be given serious consideration.

APPENDIX I

Legal Citations of State-Administered Locally-Shared Taxes Showing the Development of the Law. 1857–1929

State Statutes	Corporation Taxes	Inheritance Tax	Motor Vehicle Tax
Alabama	*Capital Stock Tax*		1911, Art. 216, p. 189
	1919, No. 328, p. 290		1915, No. 416, p. 491
	1923, No. 172, p. 164		1919, No. 328, p. 397
	1923, No. 263, p. 266		1923, No. 290, p. 285
	1927, No. 163, p. 176		
Arkansas	*Foreign Fire Ins.*		
	1921, Art. 441, p. 454		
California			1913, Ch. 326, p. 639
			1915, Ch. 188, p. 397
			1917, Ch. 213, p. 330
			1924, Ch. 266, p. 522
			1924, Ch. 266, p. 531
			1924, Ch. 266 p. 536
			p. 556
			1925, Ch. 240, p. 398
Colorado	*Foreign Fire Ins.*		1913, Ch. 114, p. 415
	1917, Ch. 75, p. 236		1919, Ch. 161, p. 533
	1919, Ch. 123, p. 414		1929, Ch. 133, p. 472
Connecticut	*Bank & Ins. Cos.*		
	1901, Ch. 106, p. 47		
	1905, Ch. 54, p. 282		
	1915, Ch. 292, p. 2134		
Florida	*Express Companies*		1911, Ch. 6212, p. 176
	1903, Ch. 5106, p. 16		1915, Ch. 6881, p. 187
	1907, Ch. 5597, p. 36		1917, Ch. 7276, p. 29
	1913, Ch. 6421, p. 19		1918, Ch. 7737, p. 48
	1914, Ch. 596, p. 236		1921, Ch. 8410, p. 47
	1920, Ch. 889, p. 594		1923, Ch. 9155, p. 153
	Telegraph Companies		1925, Ch. 10187, p. 390
	1907, Ch. 3397, p. 54		1925, Ch. 10182, p. 370
	1913, Ch. 6421, p. 50		
	1920, Ch. 986, p. 620		

APPENDIX I—*Continued*

State Statutes	Corporation Taxes	Inheritance Tax	Motor Vehicle Tax
Florida (continued)	*Railroads* 1907, Ch. 5623, p. 107		
Idaho		1929, Ch. 243, p. 469	1913, Ch. 179, p. 558 1915, Ch. 64, p. 158 1917, Ch. 52, p. 117 1919, Ch. 179, p. 65 1923, Ch. 114, p. 144 1923, Ch. 115, p. 147 1923, Ch. 63, p. 70 1925, Ch. 177, p. 315 1927, Ch. 96, p. 123 1927, Ch. 244, p. 374 1929, Ch. 195, p. 370 1929, Ch. 196, p. 372
Iowa			1911, Ch. 72, p. 69 1917, Ch. 275, p. 339 1919, Ch. 275, p. 335
Kansas	*Foreign Fire Ins.* 1895, Ch. 363, p. 534 1905, Ch. 272, p. 421 1909, Ch. 151, p. 277 1911, Ch. 204, p. 357 1921, Ch. 205, p. 329 1923, Ch. 40, p. 638	1909, Ch. 248, p. 595 1915, Ch. 357, p. 452 1917, Ch. 319, p. 469 1919, Ch. 305, p. 429 S. S. 1930, Ch. 15, p. 16	
Louisiana	*Foreign Fire Ins.* 1914, No. 295, p. 603 1924, No. 18, p. 25	1904, No. 45, p. 102 1906, No. 109, p. 173 1912, No. 42, p. 50 1918, No. 51, p. 75 1926, No. 127, p. 323	
Maine	*Railroad* 1874, Ch. 258, p. 184 1881, Ch. 91, p. 75 1891, Ch. 103, p. 111 1906, Ch. 145, p. 160 1907, Ch. 168, p. 184 1909, Ch. 81, p. 93 1911, Ch. 168, p. 181 1921, Ch. 71, p. 76 1927, Ch. 27, p. 20 *Telephone & Telegraph* 1880, Ch. 246, p. 289 1883, Ch. 213, p. 176 1891, Ch. 103, p. 110 1909, Ch. 210, p. 277 1911, Ch. 142, p. 148 1921, Ch. 72, p. 77		

APPENDIX I—*Continued*

State Statutes	Corporation Taxes	Inheritance Tax	Motor Vehicle Tax
Maryland	*Savings Banks*		1916, Ch. 687, p. 1583
	1888, Ch. 242, p. 382		
	Capital Stock Tax on Corporations		
	1914, Ch. 324, p. 506		
	1916, Ch. 604, p. 1281		
	1918, Ch. 466, p. 956		
	1927, Ch. 577, p. 1191		
Massachusetts	*Business Corporations*		
	1919, Ch. 355, p. 439		
	1920, Ch. 549, p. 547		
	1921, Ch. 375, p. 406		
	1922, Ch. 302, p. 311		
	1922, Ch. 362, p. 382		
	1922, Ch. 520, p. 632		
	1924, Ch. 206, p. 180		
	1925, Ch. 265, p. 290		
	Franchise on Public Utilities		
	1865, Ch. 283		
	1882, Ch. 13, p. 8		
	1886, Ch. 238, p. 679		
	1888, Ch. 413, p. 443		
	1898, Ch. 417, p. 359		
	1898, Ch. 578, p. 738		
	1902, Ch. 342		
	1906, Ch. 271, p. 231		
	1906, Ch. 463, p. 573, 628		
	1906, Ch. 516, p. 722		
	1908, Ch. 614, p. 731		
	1909, Ch. 490, p. 624		
	1911, Ch. 379, p. 367		
	1914, Ch. 198, p. 159		
	1916, Ch. 299, p. 325		
	1918, Ch. 257, p. 262		
	1919, Ch. 349, p. 380		
	1921, Ch. 375, p. 406		
	1921, Ch. 394, p. 467		
	1922, Ch. 520, p. 632		
	1923, Ch. 310, p. 282		
	Bank Tax		
	1925, Ch. 343, p. 417		
	1927, Ch. 223, p. 231		
	1929, Ch. 359, p. 414		
Michigan	*Steamship Companies*		1915, Ch. 302, p. 533
	1911, No. 70, p. 101		1919, Ch. 383, p. 671
			1929, Ch. 270, p. 668

APPENDIX I—*Continued*

State Statutes	Corporation Taxes	Inheritance Tax	Motor Vehicle
Minnesota	*Railroad Companies*	1905, Ch. 288, p. 427	
	1909, Ch. 454, p. 552	1911, Ch. 209, p. 274	
	1912, Ch. 9, p. 50	1911, Ch. 372, p. 516	
		1913, Ch. 455, p. 666	
	Fire Insurance Cos.	1919, Ch. 410, p. 479	
	1903, Ch. 20, p. 23	1927, Ch. 265, p. 304	
	1909, Ch. 237, p. 279		
	1919, Ch. 326, p. 342		
	Steamship Companies		
	1895, Ch. 224, p. 507		
	1919, Ch. 505, p. 677		
Mississippi			1922, Ch. 133, p.
			1924, Ch. 116, p.
			1926, Ch. 120, p.
			1928, Ch. 230, p.
Missouri	*Foreign Fire Ins. Co.*		
	1895, page 198		
	1905, page 172		
Montana		1923, Ch. 65, p. 165	1917, Ch. 75, p.
		1927, Ch. 141, p. 433	1919, Ch. 207, p.
			1921, Ch. 199, p.
			1923, Ch. 107, p.
			1927, Ch. 88, p.
			1928, Ch. 121, p.
			1929, Ch. 181, p.
			1929, Ch. 182, p.
Nebraska			1911, Ch. 115, p.
			1915, Ch. 61, p.
			1919, Ch. 190, p.
			1919, Ch. 222, p.
			1921, Ch. 278, p.
			1921, Ch. 279, p.
			1925, Ch. 159, p.
			1927, Ch. 152, p.
			1929, Ch. 145, p.
			1929, Ch. 148, p.
New Hampshire	*Rr. & Teleg. Lines*		
	1878, Ch. 62, p. 159		
	1881, Ch. 53, p. 470		
	1909, Ch. 55, p. 365		
	1911, Ch. 169, p. 225		
	Stock Fire Ins. Cos.		
	1887, Ch. 57, p. 442		
	1913, Ch. 77, p. 547		

APPENDIX I—*Continued*

State Statutes	Corporation Taxes	Inheritance Tax	Motor Vehicle Tax
New Hampshire (continued)	*Savings Banks*		
	1878, Ch. 65, p. 169		
	1889, Ch. 55, p. 76		
	1895, Ch. 108, p. 469		
	1901, Ch. 82, p. 578		
	1907, Ch. 102, p. 101		
	1911, Ch. 194, p. 256		
	1923, Ch. 72, p. 21		
	1925, Ch. 144, p. 170		
	Bldg. & Loan Assns.		
	1885, Ch. 93, p. 470		
	1903, Ch. 126, p. 129		
New Jersey	*Railroads & Canals*	1909, Ch. 228, p. 325	
	1906, Ch. 146, p. 272	1909, Ch. 238, p. 375	
	1909, Ch. 65, p. 90	1912, Ch. 226, p. 367	
	Public Utilities	1924, Ch. 57, p. 91	
	Except Railroads	1926, Ch. 294, p. 488	
	1900, Ch. 195, p. 502		
	1906, Ch. 290, p. 644		
	1917, Ch. 17, p. 43		
	1918, Ch. 239, p. 903		
	1927, Ch. 303, p. 567		
	1928, Ch. 223, p. 223		
	Addt'l Pub. Utilities		
	1919, Ch. 25, p. 51		
New Mexico	*Fire Insurance Cos.*		1923, Ch. 96, p. 100
	1905, Ch. 5, p. 13		1929, Ch. 119, p. 253
	1909, Ch. 135, p. 379		
	1915, Ch. 96, p. 141		
	1919, Ch. 175, p. 360		
	1921, Ch. 194, p. 418		
	1925, Ch. 135, p. 265		
New York	*Corporate Income Tax*		1916, Ch. 72, p. 176
	1917, Ch. 726, p. 2400		1916, Ch. 577, p. 1873
	1918, Ch. 417, p. 1259		1917, Ch. 2, p. 2
	1919, Ch. 628, p. 1658		1917, Ch. 174, p. 315
	1920, Ch. 640, p. 1633		1917, Ch. 727, p. 2412
	1921, Ch. 447, p. 1338		1917, Ch. 769, p. 2465
	1922, Ch. 654, p. 1795		1919, Ch. 472, p. 1291
	1923, Ch. 897, p. 1724		1919, Ch. 622, p. 1625
	1924, Ch. 329, p. 608		1920, Ch. 683, p. 1709
	1929, Ch. 363, p. 846		1920, Ch. 687, p. 1713
	1929, Ch. 385, p. 889		1921, Ch. 580, p. 1756
	State Banks & Trust		1922, Ch. 535, p. 1226
	Companies		1922, Ch. 317, p. 698
			1922, Ch. 17, p. 13
	1926, Ch. 286, p. 506		1922, Ch. 533, p. 1221
	1927, Ch. 477, p. 1169		1924, Ch. 360, p. 1656

APPENDIX I—*Continued*

State Statutes	Corporation Taxes	Inheritance Tax	Motor Vehicle Tax
New York (continued)	1928, Ch. 659, p. 1433 1928, Ch. 414, p. 934 *National Banks* 1926, Ch. 286, p. 518		1926, Ch. 511, p. 878 1926, Ch. 238, p. 440
North Carolina	*Bldg. & Loan Assns.* 1919, Ch. 90, p. 161 1927, Ch. 80, p. 213		
North Dakota	*Domestic & Foreign Insurance Cos.* 1887, Ch. 53, p. 153 1897, Ch. 94, p. 153 1921, Ch. 79, p. 146 1923, Ch. 66, p. 172	1917, Ch. 231, p. 320 1919, Ch. 225, p. 450 1921, Ch. 124, p. 209 1927, Ch. 267, p. 447	1911, Ch. 6, p. 7 1917, Ch. 131, p. 194 1917, Ch. 156, p. 217 1919, Ch. 44, p. 78 1925, Ch. 167, p. 204 1927, Ch. 179, p. 298
Ohio		1894, No. 715, p. 169 1913, No. 13, p. 463 1919, No. 175, p. 563 1920, No. 744, p. 1193 1923, Ch. 55, p. 26 1927, Ch. 484, p. 421 1929, Ch. 223, p. 85 1929, Ch. 497, p. 512	1919, No. 573, p. 107 1925, No. 304, p. 239 1925, No. 44, p. 301 1929, No. 104, p. 280
Oklahoma	*Foreign Fire Ins.* 1909, Ch. 21, p. 379 1913, Ch. 244, p. 678 1921, Ch. 35, p. 51		1915, Ch. 176, p. 266 1919, Ch. 290, p. 412 1925, Ch. 167, p. 269
Oregon			1913, Ch. 299, p. 572 1915, Ch. 350, p. 598 1917, Ch. 194, p. 256 1919, Ch. 399, p. 704 1920, Ch. 3, p. 46 1921, Ch. 371, p. 718 1923, Ch. 284, p. 458 1925, Ch. 327, p. 666 1925, Ch. 331, p. 674 1925, Ch. 365, p. 725 1927, Ch. 364, p. 496 1929, Ch. 360, p. 414
Pennsylvania	*Foreign Fire Ins.* 1894, Ch. 289, p. 408 1905, Ch. 166, p. 299 1919, Ch. 380, p. 964 1921, Ch. 284, p. 682 1929, Ch. 307, p. 709		
South Carolina	*Foreign Fire Ins.* 1909, No. 3, p. 7		

APPENDIX I—*Continued*

State Statutes	Corporation Taxes	Inheritance Tax	Motor Vehicle Tax
South Dakota	*Foreign & Domestic Fire Insurance*	1913, Ch. 243, p. 337	1913, Ch. 276, p. 428
	1887, Ch. 53	1915, Ch. 217, p. 419	1915, Ch. 253, p. 488
	1905, Ch. 127, p. 195	1923, Ch. 107, p. 92	1917, Ch. 302, p. 660
	1911, Ch. 184, p. 226		1919, Ch. 264, p. 309
	1913, Ch. 249, p. 363		1919, Ch. 266, p. 311
			1921, Ch. 293, p. 420
			1921, Ch. 294, p. 422
			1925, Ch. 230, p. 265
			1925, Ch. 231, p. 266
			1927, Ch. 167, p. 187
			1929, Ch. 184, p. 212
Tennessee			1919, Ch. 149, p. 546
			1929, Ch. 14, p. 26
Texas			1917, Ch. 190, p. 421
			1917, Ch. 207, p. 482
			1921, Ch. 52, p. 167
			1923, Ch. 75, p. 155
			1927, Ch. 162, p. 235
			S. S. 1929, Ch. 88, p. 172
Washington	*Bank Tax*		1915, Ch. 142, p. 385
	1929, Ch. 151, p. 380		1917, Ch. 155, p. 633
			1919, Ch. 46, p. 90
			1919, Ch. 54, p. 108
			1921, Ch. 96, p. 264
			1923, Ch. 181, p. 595
			1926, Ch. 185, p. 562
Wisconsin	*Foreign Fire Ins.*	1903, Ch. 44, p. 65	
	1926, Ch. 89, p. 579	1905, Ch. 96, p. 162	
	Telephone Companies	1909, Ch. 509, p. 645	
	1905, Ch. 448, p. 842	1913, Ch. 627, p. 779	
	1909, Ch. 535, p. 739	1915, Ch. 253, p. 257	
	1911, Ch. 651, p. 603	1921, Ch. 658, p. 946	
	1927, Ch. 306, p. 344	1923, Ch. 306, p. 506	
	Street Railways	1925, Ch. 249, p. 327	
	1905, Ch. 493, p. 871	1927, Ch. 416, p. 513	
	1915, Ch. 526, p. 696	1929, Ch. 298, p. 66	
	1917, Ch. 667, p. 1196		
	1925, Ch. 441, p. 638		
	Corporation Income (See Personal Income)		
Wyoming	*Express Companies*		
	1903, Ch. 111, p. 146		
	1907, Ch. 61, p. 73		

APPENDIX I—*Continued*

State Statutes	Gasoline Taxes	Common Carrier Tax	Personal Income Tax
Alabama	1923, No. 162, p. 36 1923, No. 172, p. 197 1927, No. 5, p. 16 1927, No. 310, p. 326		
Arizona	1921, No. 116, p. 250 1923, No. 35, p. 225 1929, No. 312-3, p. 524		
California	1923, Ch. 267, p. 571 1925, Ch. 359, p. 659 1927, Ch. 716, p. 1309 1927, Ch. 795, p. 1565	1923, Ch. 341, p. 706 1925, Ch. 412, p. 833	
Colorado	1919, Ch. 168, p. 566 1923, Ch. 153, p. 474 1927, Ch. 140, p. 530 1929, Ch. 139, p. 488	1927, Ch. 135, p. 502 1927, Ch. 134, p. 515 1929, Ch. 135, p. 474	
Connecticut		1927, Ch. 268, p. 4328 1929, Ch. 229, p. 4660	
Florida	1923, Ch. 9120, p. 27 1925, Ch. 10025, p. 12 1927, Ch. 12037, p. 327 1929, Ch. 14575, p. 1121 1929, Ch. 14576, p. 1125 1929, Ch. 14577, p. 1125	1929, Ch. 13700, p. 348	
Georgia	1923, Ch. 2, p. 41 1925, Ch. 436, p. 66 1925, Ch. 399, p. 68 1927, Ch. 378, p. 104 1929, Ch. 284, p. 99		
Illinois	1927, No. 499, p. 758 S.S. 1928, No. 1, p. 88 1929, No. 85, p. 625		
Indiana	1923, Ch. 182, p. 532 1925, Ch. 146, p. 367 1929, Ch. 48, p. 102		
Iowa	1925, Ch. 6, p. 10 Code 1927, Ch. 251, p. 667 1925, Ch. 274, p. 355	1923, Ch. 97, p. 93 1925, Ch. 4, p. 3	
Kansas	1927, Ch. 255, p. 460 1928, Ch. 4, p. 3 1929, Ch. 287, p. 459 1929, Ch. 225, p. 389	1925, Ch. 206, p. 269	

APPENDIX I—*Continued*

State Statutes	Gasoline Taxes	Common Carrier Tax	Personal Income Tax
Kentucky		1924, Ch. 79, p. 200	
		1926, Ch. 111, p. 356	
Maryland	1927, Ch. 327, p. 583	1916, Ch. 714, p. 1666	
	1929, Ch. 96, p. 192	1918, Ch. 304, p. 704	
		1922, Ch. 401, p. 885	
		1924, Ch. 291, p. 851	
		1927, Ch. 152, p. 246	
Massachusetts			1916, Ch. 269, p. 249
			1918, Ch. 32, p. 23
			1918, Ch. 20, p. 97
			1918, Ch. 219, p. 186
			1919, Ch. 314, p. 296
			1919, Ch. 363, p. 469
			1920, Ch. 352, p. 370
			1922, Ch. 376, p. 449
			1922, Ch. 54, p. 38
			1923, Ch. 287, p. 260
			1923, Ch. 378, p. 389
			1924, Ch. 351, p. 318
Michigan	1927, Ch. 150, p. 228		
	1929, Ch. 157, p. 444		
Mississippi	1922, Ch. 116, p. 102		
	1924, Ch. 115, p. 108		
	1926, Ch. 119, p. 185		
	1928, Ch. 198, p. 266		
	S.S. 1928, Ch. 21, p. 31		
Nebraska	1929, Ch. 166, p. 572		
Nevada		1925, Ch. 162, p. 247	
		1927, Ch. 185, p. 326	
New Hampshire			1923, Ch. 65, p. 78
			1929, Ch. 32, p. 43
New York	1929, Ch. 364, p. 846		1919, Ch. 627, p. 1636
			1920, Ch. 691, p. 1720
			1920, Ch. 694, p. 1729
			1921, Ch. 477, p. 1431
			1921, Ch. 625, p. 1948
			1922, Ch. 107, p. 400
			1922, Ch. 425, p. 906
			1922, Ch. 671
			1923, Ch. 897, p. 1734
			1923, Ch. 137, p. 164
			1924, Ch. 27, p. 28

APPENDIX I—*Continued*

State Statutes	Gasoline Taxes	Common Carrier Tax	Personal Income Tax
New York (continued)			1926, Ch. 208, p. 382 1926, Ch. 288, p. 534 1926, Ch. 366, p. 646 1926, Ch. 543, p. 939 1928, Ch. 239, p. 482
North Carolina	1929, Ch. 40, p. 33		
North Dakota	1929, Ch. 166, p. 208		
Ohio	1925, No. 44, p. 294 1929, No. 104, p. 278 1929, No. 335, p. 70	1923, No. 474, p. 211 1929, No. 141, p. 482	
Oklahoma	1923, Ch. 239, p. 409 1924, Ch. 101, p. 116 1925, Ch. 373, p. 198 1929, Ch. 278, p. 401		
Oregon		1925, Ch. 380, p. 756 1929, Ch. 374, p. 509	
Pennsylvania	1921, Ch. 368, p. 1021 1923, Ch. 318, p. 834 1925, Ch. 362, p. 671 1927, Ch. 159, p. 201 1927, Ch. 167, p. 294 1929, Ch. 405, p. 1037		
South Carolina	1922, Ch. 494, p. 835 1923, Ch. 146, p. 205 1925, Ch. 34, p. 53 1927, Ch. 73, p. 136 1928, Ch. 574, p. 1089 1929, Ch. 101, p. 105 1929, Ch. 102, p. 107	1925, Ch. 170, p. 252 1928, Ch. 663, p. 1238 1929, Ch. 220, p. 247	
Tennessee		1918, Ch. 71, p. 158 1919, Ch. 116, p. 174	1929, Ch. 86; 116, p. S.S. 1929, Ch. 16, p.
Texas		1918, Ch. 71, p. 158 S.S. 1929, Ch. 88, p. 172	
Virginia	1923, Ch. 107, p. 125 1926, Ch. 137, p. 238 1928, Ch. 174, p. 606 1928, Ch. 462, p. 1169 1928, Ch. 485, p. 1274	1923, Ch. 161, p. 195 1924, Ch. 222, p. 330 1926, Ch. 551, p. 920	
Washington	1929, Ch. 88, p. 161		

APPENDIX I—*Continued*

State Statutes	Gasoline Taxes	Common Carrier Tax	Personal Income Tax
Wisconsin			1911, Ch. 658, p. 984
			1913, Ch. 615, p. 767
			1913, Ch. 554, p. 626
			1913, Ch. 720, p. 1004
			1917, Ch. 161, p. 284
			1917, Ch. 246, p. 418
			1917, Ch. 485, p. 800
			1919, Ch. 147, p. 153
			1919, Ch. 435, p. 628
			1919, Ch. 461, p. 698
			1919, Ch. 667, p. 1163
			1921, Ch. 65, p. 110
			1921, Ch. 311, p. 458
			1921, Ch. 335, p. 480
			1922, Ch. 310, p. 811
			1923, Ch. 318, p. 521
			1925, Ch. 57, p. 116
			1925, Ch. 146, p. 650
			1927, Ch. 539, p. 899
Wyoming	1929, Ch. 139, p. 228		

APPENDIX I—*Continued*

State Statutes	Miscellaneous Taxes	Forest Tax	Severance Tax
Alabama		1923, No. 486, p. 639	
Arizona	*State Road Fund* 1912, Ch. 68, p. 332 S.S. 1912, Ch. 66, p. 188 1913, Ch. 7, p. 1659 S.S. 1915, Ch. 7, p. 121 1921, Ch. 57, p. 157 1922, No. 35, p. 239 1923, No. 156, p. 199		
Arkansas	*Mining Records* 1895, Ch. 88, p. 116		1923, Ch. 118, p. 67 1929, Ch. 283, p. 1187
Connecticut	*Unincorporated Business* 1925, Ch. 114, p. 3883 *Choses in Action* 1915, Ch. 293, p. 2140 1917, Ch. 243, p. 2391 1923, Ch. 190, p. 3615 1925, Ch. 43, p. 34		
Idaho		1929, Ch. 185, p. 329	
Indiana		1921, pp. 1071-6	
Iowa	*Cigarette Tax* 1927, Ch. 33, p. 26		
Kansas	*Secured Debts* 1927, Ch. 326, p. 531 1929, Ch. 293, p. 467		
Louisiana		1926, Ch. 120, p. 187	1922, No. 140, p. 304 1926, No. 301, p. 569 1928, No. 5, p. 6
Maine	*Dog Licenses* 1893, Ch. 287, p. 340 1897, Ch. 297, p. 332 1901, Ch. 163, p. 174 1909, Ch. 222, p. 295		
Massachusetts	*Boxing Fees* 1920, Ch. 619, p. 692		
Michigan		1925, Ch. 94, p. 126 1927, Ch. 86, p. 121	1929, Ch. 48, p. 85

APPENDIX I—*Concluded*

State Statutes	Miscellaneous Taxes	Forest Tax	Severance Tax
Montana		1927, Ch. 35, p. 855	1923, Ch. 67, p. 174
New York	*Billiard and Poolroom Licenses* 1922, Ch. 671, p. 1834 1928, Ch. 90, p. 238 *Real Estate Brokers' Licenses* 1922, Ch. 672, p. 1834 1927, Ch. 107, p. 418		
North Dakota	*Billiard and Poolroom Licenses* 1921, Ch. 84, p. 151 1923, Ch. 293, p. 341		
Oklahoma			1915, Ch. 107, p. 151 1916, Ch. 39, p. 102 1927, Ch. 55, p. 76
South Dakota	*Money and Credit* 1919, Ch. 109, p. 91 1923, Ch. 108, p. 93		
Vermont	*Peddlers' Licenses* 1857, No. 19 1862, Ch. 81 1886, Ch. 92 1894, Ch. 198 1904, Ch. 145, p. 203 1912, Ch. 61, p. 63 1921, Ch. 43, p. 42 1925, Ch. 31, p. 151 1929, Ch. 168, p. 32		
Wisconsin		1927, Ch. 454, p. 659 1929, Ch. 343, p. 75	

BIBLIOGRAPHY

General Works

American Bankers Association, *A Survey of Bank Taxation in the United States,* New York, September, 1929.

Bastable, C. F., *Public Finance,* London, 1903.

Beard, C. A., *American Government and Politics,* New York, 1910.

Blachly, F. F. and Oatman, N., *The Government and Administration of Germany,* Maryland, 1928.

Bryce, James, *The American Commonwealth,* New York, 1922.

Comstock, Alzada, *State Taxation of Personal Incomes,* New York, 1921.

Dillon, John F., *Commentaries on the Law of Municipal Corporations,* Boston, 1911.

Fairlie, John A., *Local Government in Counties, Towns and Villages,* New York, 1906.

Grice, J. Watson, *National and Local Finance,* London, 1910.

Haig, Robert Murray, *The Public Finances of Post-War France,* New York, 1929.

Kendrick, M. Slade, *The Collection of Taxes by the State of New York, and the Division of these Revenues with Units of Local Government,* New York, 1930.

Leland, Simeon E., *The Classified Property Tax,* New York, 1928.

Lutz, Harley L., *Public Finance,* New York, 1924.

Lutz, Harley L., *The State Tax Commission,* Harvard University Press, Cambridge, 1918.

Maxey, Chester C., *County Administration,* New York, 1919.

Maxey, Chester C., *Outline of Municipal Government,* New York, 1924.

McBain, Howard L., *American City Progress and the Public Law,* Columbia University Press, New York, 1918.

McBain, Howard L., *The Law and the Practice of Municipal Home Rule,* Columbia University Press, New York, 1916.

Motor Vehicle Conference Committee, *Special Taxation for Motor Vehicles,* New York, 1930.

National Industrial Conference Board, Inc., *Cost of Government in The United States, 1927-1928,* New York, 1930.

National Municipal Review, Washington, September, 1929.

National Tax Association, *Bulletin,* vols. xxiv-xliii (inc.), New York, 1921-1929.

National Tax Association, *Proceedings in State and Local Finance,* vols. i-xxii, 1907-1929.

Newcomer, Mabel, *Separation of State and Local Revenue in the United States*, New York, 1917.
Porter, Kirk H., *County and Township Government in the United States*, New York, 1922.
Political Science Quarterly, M. Newcomer, *Tendencies in State and Local Finance and their relation to State and Local Functions*, vol. xliii, no. 1, March, 1928.
Seligman, Edwin R. A., *Essays in Taxation*, New York, 1925.
Seligman, Edwin R. A., *The Income Tax*, New York, 1911.
Shirras, G. Findlay, *The Science of Public Finance*, New York, 1924.
Webb, Sidney, *Grants in Aid: A Criticism and a Proposal*, London, 1920.

REPORTS OF FEDERAL OFFICIALS

Bureau of the Census—*Digest of State Laws Relating to Taxation and Revenue*, Washington, 1925; *Financial Statistics of States*, 1927, *Preliminary Report*, 1928; *Twelfth Census of the United States*, Washington, 1900; *Statistical Abstract*, 1903; *Wealth, Debt and Taxation*, Special Report, Washington, 1907; *Wealth, Debt and Taxation*, vol. ii, part iv, Washington, 1913.
Bureau of Public Roads—*Total Local Road Income and Funds Available*, Washington, 1928; *Local Roads, Disbursements*, Washington, 1928.
Forest Service—Progress Report of the Forest Taxation Inquiry, F. R. Fairchild; *Digest of State Forest Tax Laws Enacted or Revised During the Calendar Year 1929*, Washington, March 15, 1930.
Report of the Agent General for Reparation Payments, Berlin, November 30, 1926; London, July 1, 1929.
Statesman's Yearbook—London, 1930.

STATE STATUTES AND REPORTS OF STATE OFFICIALS

Alabama
State Statutes—1903-1927.
State Auditor—*Report*, 1928.
Arizona
State Statutes—1912-1929.
State Auditor—*Report*, 1926-28.
Arkansas
State Statutes—1895-1929.
State Auditor—*Report*, 1927-1928.
California
State Statutes—1923-1929.
Final Report of the California Tax Commission, 1929.
Colorado
State Statutes—1913-1929.
State Auditor—*Biennial Report*, 1926-1928.

Connecticut
State Statutes—1901-1929.
Treasurer—*Report*, 1929.
Florida
State Statutes—1903-1929
Comptroller of the State—*Report*, 1928
Georgia
State Statutes—1921-1929.
Comptroller General—*Report*, 1928.
Idaho
State Statutes—1908-1929.
State Auditor—*Report*, 1927-1928.
Illinois
State Statutes—1927-1929.
Auditor—*Report*, 1928.
Indiana
State Statutes—1921-1929.
State Auditor—*Report*, 1928.
Iowa
State Statutes—1894-1929.
Auditor—*Report*, 1928.
Kansas
State Statutes—1895-1929.
State Auditor—*Report*, 1927-1928.
Kentucky
State Statutes—1924-1929.
Auditor of Public Accounts—*Report*, 1930.
Louisiana
State Statutes—1904-1929.
State Auditor—*Report*, 1926-1927.
Maine
State Statutes—1874-1929.
State Auditor—*Report*, 1928.
Maryland
State Statutes—1888-1929.
Comptroller of the Treasury—*Report*, 1928.
Massachusetts
State Statutes—1882-1929.
Commission of Corporations and Taxation—*Report*, 1928.
Michigan
State Statutes—1911-1929.
Auditor General—*Report*, 1928.
Minnesota
State Statutes—1895-1929.
Biennial Report of State Auditor—*Report*, 1928.

Mississippi
State Statutes—1914-1929.
Missouri
State Statutes—1895-1929.
State Auditor—*Report*, 1927-1928.
Montana
State Statutes—1897-1929.
State Auditor—*Biennial Report*, 1927-1929.
Nebraska
State Statutes—1911-1929.
Auditor of Public Accounts—*Report*, 1928.
Nevada
State Statutes—1925-1929.
State Comptroller—*Report*, 1928.
New Hampshire
State Statutes—1878-1929.
State Treasurer—*Report*, 1929.
New Jersey
State Statutes—1888-1929.
Comptroller—*Report*, 1928.
State Board of Taxes—*Report*, 1928.
New Mexico
State Statutes—1897-1929.
Comptroller—*Report*, 1927-1928.
New York
Federal and State Tax Systems—1930.
New York State Joint Legislative Committee on Taxation and Retrenchment—Albany, 1922.
Special Report State Tax Commission—*Fiscal Problems of Rural Decline*, R. T. Comptom, Albany, 1930.
State Statutes—1910-1929.
State Tax Commission—*Report*, Albany, 1927-1928.
New York State Legislative Department—compiled by Beulah Bailey.
Compilation of Laws of State Taxes Referring to Mortgage Registration Tax—1926.
Digest of State Laws of Various States on Taxation of Forests—1926.
Digest of Taxes and Fees on Motor Vehicle Operation—1930.
Digest of Cigarette Laws (unpublished)—1927.
North Carolina
State Statutes—1919-1929.
State Tax Commission—*Report*, 1928.
North Dakota
State Statutes—1911-1929.
Tax Commissioner—*Report*, 1928.

Ohio
State Statutes—1894-1929.
Auditor of the State—*Report*, 1928.
Oklahoma
State Statutes—1909-1929.
Auditor of the State—*Report*, 1928.
Oregon
State Statutes—1911-1929.
Secretary of State—*Report*, 1927-1928.
State Tax Commission—*Report*, 1927-1928.
Pennsylvania
State Statutes—1905-1929.
Budget of the Commonwealth—1929.
South Carolina
State Statutes—1909-1929.
Comptroller General—*Report*, 1928.
South Dakota
State Statutes—1903-1929.
State Auditor—*Report*, 1928.
Tennessee
State Statutes—1917-1929.
Commission of Finance and Taxation—*Report*, 1928.
Texas
State Statutes—1917-1929.
Comptroller of Public Accounts—*Report*, 1928.
Vermont
State Statutes—1862-1929.
Treasurer—*Report*, 1928.
Virginia
State Statutes—1915-1929.
State Comptroller—*Report*, 1929.
Washington
State Statutes—1915-1929.
State Auditor—*Report*, 1929.
Wisconsin
State Statutes—1883-1929.
Wisconsin Tax Commission—*Report of State and Local Taxes*, 1901-1928.
Wyoming
State Statutes—1903-1929.
State Auditor—*Report*, 1928.

INDEX

I

K

L

M

N

O

Bei Fragen zur Produktsicherheit wenden Sie sich bitte an:
If you have any questions regarding product safety,
please contact:

Walter de Gruyter GmbH
Genthiner Straße 13
10785 Berlin
productsafety@degruyterbrill.com